Food and travels Asia
Alastair Hendy

Tourist

Food and travels Asia
Alastair Hendy

MITCHELL BEAZLEY

Food and travels Asia
by Alastair Hendy

First published in Great Britain in 2004 by Mitchell Beazley,
an imprint of Octopus Publishing Group Limited, 2–4 Heron
Quays, London E14 4JP.
© Octopus Publishing Group Limited 2004
Text & photography © Alastair Hendy 2004

ISBN 1 84000 907 1
A CIP catalogue record for this book is available from the
British Library.

Design Direction and Photography: Alastair Hendy

Commissioning Editor: Rebecca Spry
Executive Art Editor: Yasia Williams
Senior Designer: Tim Pattinson
Editing: Susan Fleming
Proofreading: Diona Gregory
Production: Sarah Rogers
Index: John Noble

Typeset in Magda and Din
Printed and bound by Toppan Printing Company, China

For John

Asia

Introduction 6

India 8

Burma (Myanmar) 34

Thailand 76

Laos 120

Vietnam 152

Singapore 192

Bali 214

Asia Basics 236

Picture captions 238

Index 239

Thanks 240

InÉroduction

Q: Where on Earth do you find the best food?

A: Difficult, that one. Because you find the best in the most unlikely places, and alongside the worst. And your best is also about time and place, the mood you're in and who you're with. Many many things. Simplicity is usually the key though. The humble evokes memories — and joy: fat barbecued prawns off the most meagre of fires on a beach in Trivandrum, India; a snack of sliced boiled potato, sev (crisp noodles), green mango, chopped onion and tomato smothered in mango chutney-sweetened tamarind, known as bhel puri, had off an old knocked-about tin plate amid the evening magic of Bombay's Juhu beach; sucking on chilli crab in a Burmese hut with the dingiest of light bulbs; a bowl of cao lau from a hawker in Hoi An, Vietnam — a mulch of glorious noodley things, eaten while balanced on a doll-sized stool at a pavement table amid the furore of chatter, steam and the comings-and-goings of fellow diners; grilled lime-stung octopus had under a sky full of shooting stars on a desolate beach with friends... and so much more. Get me? We just love our food, in its place. **Q: Where do you find the best places?** A: If you mean out-of-this-world places, they're all out there. The most romantic and beautiful are not only in the far-flung corners of the planet, but can also be found, say, at a hawker's stall on a busy street corner in diesel-blown Bangkok or in the incense-spun calm of one of the city's Chinese temples. You won't find them in a swanky hotel, no matter how much it has 'taken its inspiration from the natives, blah, blah'. They're there to take your dosh. Nothing wrong in that, but money never buys it for me. The best places take you by surprise. And sometimes in the most surprising of places. Asia's really taken off. Low-budget air fares and increased flights; TV, radio and travel magazines; food trends and eating out; and an interest in the cultures, ingredients and dishes from the Far East have crept into our lives. Many of us have sampled a week or two in India or Thailand. If you can't go, I want to take you there. There's a taste too of the less-travelled places in Indochina, such as Laos, and there's Burma (now Myanmar) too. This book is about all our travels: the ones we can take from the comfort of our chair, at home, or on a jet plane, for real. **All recipes serve 4.**

India

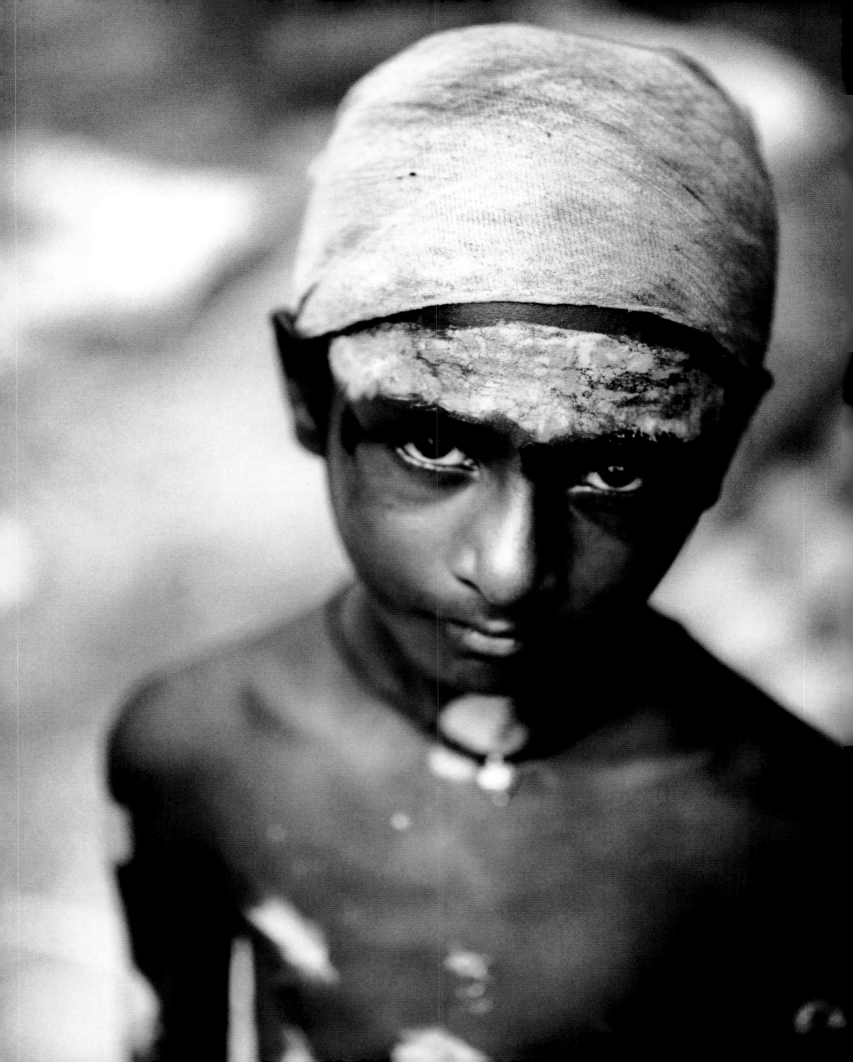

India
flavours

Nowhere else in the world will you find so many powders, resins, seeds, twigs, dried things, and fresh things to flavour food. India is the spice queen of Asia; spices the trillion jewels in its crown. And I don't mean chilli. Flavours, not heat. Things like coriander, cumin, fenugreek, fennel, poppy and radhuni (mustard), black and green cardamom, nutmeg, cinnamon, clove and curry leaves. Masalas (specific spice blends for specific dishes) are used, for there's no such things as curry powder in India. This is Western nomenclature. North and south divide India's food. Bread, or roti, is the staple of the cooler north; rice the backbone of the more tropical south. Fish is the stuff of the coast. Food is designed for spiritual well-being as well as for the stomach. And spiritual purity is believed to attain loftier heights in vegetarianism. Jains, Buddhists and Brahmin Hindus are extra picky, believing certain foods pure and sacred. Muslims and Parsees have fewer taboos, and eat most stuff, including everything on four legs, unless of course it is a pig. Meat is scarce, vegetables plentiful, so most are vegetarian and do beautiful things with the most ordinary of produce.

A brace of blue-backed prawns, the size of
lobsters, whistle and jump among baby garlic
cloves in a hot pan

It's in a little wooden shack, down by Cochin's fishing nets, where I and fork find Keralan heaven: flakes of fish buried like treasure under a pilaf of cardamom-fragrant rice, spotted with nuts and fruit, and pin-pricked with pepper. The hut is all palm thatch and compressed earth floor. It's no restaurant. It has its share of over-friendly flies and a collection of patio plastic chairs. It's real. And its owners, Saji and his wife Mumthaz, dish up real food.

There are two gas burners, a hand-pumped washing-up basin and a zinc-topped work table, scarred by the toil of filleting. Well-scoured aluminium pots, pans and strainers and enormous serving platters gleam through a smoke and steam haze. Two light bulbs barely light the way. A brace of blue-backed prawns, the size of lobsters, whistle and jump among baby garlic cloves in a hot pan, their coconut oil-rubbed carapaces chameleoning to brittle pink. A bowl of fresh coconut, mustard seed and chilli chutney beams on the side. A boy rubs a pearl spot fish with a cumin and turmeric chilli paste, another rinses and rattles turquoise-rimmed mussels in the sink, while a third darts about with the orders. Mumthaz works with dexterity, barely moving in her sari, and lets fall crumbled curry leaves, fronds of coral-like mace and shrivelled black grapes into a blackened pot that holds her glorious red snapper pullao (pilaff). The whole shack shimmies in a rainbow of spice.

I'd found my India. Here in the old colonial Dutch town of Fort Cochin, Kerala. In a hut on the tropical Malabar Coast, overlooking an ancient seaport. All the spice, history and seafood of the place was here, right under – and up – my nose. I can eat, bask in, and watch a whole devourable world go by, as Mumthaz beavers away behind me, now perched side-saddle on a low metal seat, grating half-shell coconuts on a lethal looking serrated spike.

A stone's throw away, beyond a tree baubled with tamarind pods, is a crowd watching a turbaned gentleman bullying a cobra to rise from its biscuit-tin-sized basket. And, beyond a line of fish stalls, strung out along the bay, like a slice from Costner's failed Waterworld, are Cochin's 13th-century Chinese fishing nets, built by forgotten sea-breezing traders from the court of Kublai Khan. From the lines of lashed wooden poles, thick braided coir ropes and boulder-weighted pulley systems, hang a web of nets over the waters of the Malabar mudbanks. The massive contraptions creak as they flex on their wobbly jetty legs, ladling up a wriggling mass of breakwater fish.

It's here I'd bought my fish before taking it to the fish-fryer huts. This is where Saji's boys will woo anyone – if bearing a plastic bag of fish – and then cook it, for around 30 rupees, to instruction. I choose from a mass of coloured washing-up bowls filled with aquarium-like Athena fish; steely fry and silvery mullet; inky baskets of speckled squid; more turquoise mussels and more fat blue prawns with angle-poise claws; and then get side-tracked by a frenzy of cuttlefish activity. A mass of the things with zebra-striped backs, all frills and stuck tentacles, are tipped on to an ink-tarred tarpaulin thrown down at my feet, instantly a flip-flopped ring of brown feet joins mine and the lot is auctioned, and scooped back up, all within seconds.

The morning had started at Broadway fruit and veg market, along Canal Street on mainland Cochin. Most of the stuff arrives from the neighbouring state of Tamil Nadu – India's big vegetable plot – and the early morning unloading of trucks is frantic. Skinny legs with bandy gaits scoot top-heavy loads on padded heads from truck to stallholder. Stallholders are focused, arranging rolled-down sacks and baskets with bitter gourds, aubergine and green finger spirals of okra, stacking pineapples into pyramids and hooking up lengths of red bananas. There's a fish area, a spice and rice alley, and a knife sellers' street. And to keep everyone's cogs rolling and watered, a tea wallah purveys tea from a bicycle, strapped with rear-mounted urn and a handle-bar-swinging teapot. Kerala is a lush strip of land on India's most south-western tip, its borders buffered by the Lakshadweep Sea and the Western Ghats – hills forested with teak, rosewood, ebony and cardamom and tea plantations. My first few days I spend up in these hills, between Admilly and Munnar. It is the end of November, summer's hot monsoons have dissipated, and the air is still balmy, yet fresh. I'm met at Cochin's airport by a Mr Vareesh and I am hot. A close hot. Arrivals and customs smelt spicy. A polished cream-and-chrome-trimmed 1950s Ambassador awaits and I dive into the sanctuary of the well-worn soft backseat. Dazed and confused I doze through a heat and haze of exhaust as our car inches its way to Cochin in a traffic-jammed cavalcade of vegetable trucks, bikes, Ambassadors, animals and some interesting whiffs. After a lassi and thali, we head west to the cool sanctuary of the hills.

First stop is the Tripunithura Hindu temple, where elephants munch in holy silence on sugar palm, their keepers at their feet. A Hindu festival, to last the week, begins and quiet turns to clamour. The animals are decked in gold head-plates, with riders aloft holding dainty umbrellas, round fans and pom-pom paraphernalia. Oil lamps flame and elephants sway. At each blast of clarinet, cymbal, drum and trumpet their keepers make finger contact to pressure points on their pet's ankles, keeping them soothed and perhaps mindful to where they may plonk a foot and five tons of weight. Then I move on up into the Cardamom Hills.

And I return to Cochin, back to where I began, outside Saji's hut. The day's fading, the water's turned to gold and the snake charmer's packed up shop. An elderly couple, she in scarlet cloth and he with grey hippy hair, play a tune on bamboo windpipes next to me. Apart from the breath of a breeze catching the hem of her sari, their slim fingers skipping over the flutes are the only things that move. The fishing nets are a picture postcard; Mumthaz is doing something wonderful with mussels, chilli and ginger, and the masala whiff of crispy fish and lime is telling me it's time to eat. Supper's up

Seafood and spice

Chutney thali

Excellent starter this. Quick. And you can make it as no-cook as you want – yet it will look like you've slaved. Assemble it in small bowls, on leaves (if you want arty) or in dishes set on small trays or on extra large plates. Poppadums are essential. Pooris (small flat breads), fried until they puff and go crisp, can be bought ready-made. (See left).

Yoghurt dip: beat 500g chilled yoghurt with 1 crushed garlic clove and a handful of chopped mint.

Red onion salad: slice 1 red onion very finely into rings, and then toss it with salt and pepper, 2 tbsp lemon juice and 1/2 tsp dried chilli flakes. Halve, de-seed and chop up 1 tomato and toss this in too, along with a handful of roughly chopped leaves and stems of fresh coriander. Leave for a good half hour or more before serving.

Green chutney: pulse-blast 1/2 bunch each of coriander and mint with 4 de-seeded green chillies, 1 tsp caster sugar and a squeeze of lemon juice.

Spiced mango dip: purée 1 ripe mango with 3 tablespoons hot mango chutney.

Bought sweet mango chutney and pickles. Fried poppadums or pooris.

Coconut and mint chutney

This won't keep like a regular chutney, so use it up. The easiest way to split a coconut is to double-bag it inside two carrier bags, twist them shut then, holding everything firmly, slam the package on to a hard surface such as the pavement. You can make this as coarse or as chunky as you like – just chop everything according to your taste. I'd pound about a third of the ingredients to something paste-like in a mortar first, then toss this through the rest – it's a textural thing, and not essential. In India they'd use kakris, a skinless, seedless cucumber.

4 tbsp freshly grated coconut or desiccated coconut
1 tbsp vegetable oil
2 small hot dried chillies, chopped
2 tsp mustard seeds
1 tsp fenugreek seeds
1/2 apple, cored and chopped
4cm piece cucumber, chopped
small bunch of mint, chopped
lemon or lime juice to taste
salt

If using a fresh coconut, save some of its watery 'milk'. Heat the oil in a frying pan, add the chillies and spices and fry for 20-30 seconds or until they waft fragrant. Scrape the spice, seeds and oil from the pan over the grated coconut and mix with the remaining prepared ingredients. Add reserved coconut milk to moisten if you have some, then taste, adding more lemon or lime juice and salt if it needs it.

Chandrika's garlic pickle

Chandrika K. Ganatra, 'specialist in dinner rolls, squashes, Punjabi dishes and pickles' says her card. She takes me bare-foot across a floor tiled in blue and terracotta and sits me at her table. Spices, mangoes and a Pandora's box of unfamiliar ingredients sit in neat rows upon the patterned plastic cloth. Her bracelets jangle as she flutters her hands over bowls of saffron and cardamom syrup. Then I taste her pickle – made with the smallest of green mangoes, weeny cloves of garlic massaged with salt, turmeric, hing (a powdered resin, asafoetida), mustard powder, ground methi seeds (fenugreek) and chilli, and moistened with oil and a dab of castor oil. It's a winner.

2 unripe green mangoes, or 6 unwaxed lemons/limes, washed
2 tbsp groundnut oil
1 tsp ground turmeric
1/2 tsp asafoetida (optional)
3 tbsp coursely ground mustard seeds
1 tbsp coursely ground fenugreek seeds
1 tbsp red chilli powder
1 head garlic (preferably small cloves), separated into cloves and peeled
3 tbsp salt 1/2

Cut the mangoes or lemons or limes into small chunks, leaving the skin on and discard the mango stones. Heat the oil with all the spices until it wafts fragrant, then toss through the chunks of fruit, garlic and the salt, and remove from the heat. Put the mixture into a lidded container (such as a jar), then leave it in a coolish place for about 10 days. Try and remember to turn it upside down every now and then to give everything a fresh coating of the mix. It will keep refrigerated for a couple of months or so.

Malabar fish pilaff with raisins, cardamom, pepper and mace

This will put the Cardamom Hills and Kerala's fishing nets on your plate. Throwing spices into a pan of hot oil lets you visit a world without having to step on a plane. A cloud of exotics – liquorice and molasses, allspice leaves and betel nuts – as if blown in from the Malabar Banks, will steep you in India; the perfume of narcotic nuances working wonders on everything it touches. (See left).

6 tbsp sunflower oil
100g shelled cashew nuts
2 onions, 1 finely sliced, 1 finely chopped
1 tsp each cumin seeds and roughly crushed black
  peppercorns
3 pieces cassia bark or 1 cinnamon stick
8 cardamom pods, bruised
3 pieces whole mace
2cm piece fresh root ginger, peeled and grated
3 cloves garlic, crushed
500g basmati rice, thoroughly rinsed in cold water
  and drained
salt and pepper
600g fish fillets, such as snapper, sea bream or
  red mullet
2 tbsp fat raisins
100ml coconut milk

Heat 2 tbsp of oil in a large casserole and lightly brown the nuts on all sides. Drain on kitchen roll. Fry the sliced onion in the same oil until dark brown and caramelized, then drain and reserve. Add the cumin, pepper, cassia, cardamom and mace to the oil (adding a drop more if needed) and gently fry for 30 seconds, or until you can smell the aroma – don't burn them. Stir in the chopped onion, ginger and garlic and gently fry until the onion has softened. Tip the rice into the pan and turn through with the spiced onion to coat. Add enough water to cover the rice by 2cm, salt it, then cover and bring to the boil. Turn down the heat to very low and simmer for 6 minutes. Turn off the heat and leave covered for 10 minutes. Meanwhile, heat 2 more tbsp oil in a non-stick frying pan. Rub the fish with salt and a few grinds of pepper and fry skin-side down for 1 minute, then remove and drain. They won't be cooked, just crisped. Bed down the fillets in the rice pan so they're layered into the rice and covered up, interspersing the layers with the raisins, nuts and caramelized sliced onion. Make holes in the rice with the handle of a wooden spoon, then pour over the coconut milk. Cover and put in a 180°C/350°F/Gas 4 oven for 30 minutes.

Keralan mussels with ginger and chilli

You can turn this into something creamy-soupy – moules marinière meets India – by bubbling in a dash of coconut milk after you've turned through the mussels.

1kg net mussels
2 shallots, finely chopped
2 cloves garlic, finely chopped
salt and pepper
1 tbsp vegetable oil
1 tsp paprika
3 red mild chillies, deseeded and
  roughly chopped
4cm piece fresh root ginger, peeled and
  roughly chopped
small bunch of fresh coriander, chopped

Rinse and scrub the mussels. Discard any that remain open. Fry the shallots and garlic with salt and pepper in the oil until the shallots start to pick up flecks of colour. Stir in the paprika, half the chillies and half the ginger and fry for a further minute. Add a dash of water and reduce to a paste-like sauce. Add the mussels, and the remaining chilli and ginger and turn to coat the mussels with spice mixture. Cover, turn up the heat and steam-fry for 2 minutes, or until the mussels have opened. Discard those that remain shut. Dish up with lots of chopped coriander strewn over.

PRAWN AND MANGO CURRY, PAGE 33

Jaisalmer lassi with saffron ice-cream

In the far-flung reaches of the Thar Desert in Rajasthan sits Jaisalmer, a maze of sandstone alleys and homes in a sun-baked medieval fort that tolls with Jain temple bells at every dawn. A little dairy, a parlour with a few benches and some hand-cranked freezers, serves up saffroned lassis bobbing with kulfi and dotted with candied peel. Makes pudding the stuff of dreams.

650ml milk
a good pinch of saffron, infused in 1 tbsp hot water
16 cardamom pods, seeds only, bashed
230g caster sugar, plus 2 tbsp
6 free-range egg yolks
1kg Greek yoghurt
300ml double cream, whipped to soft peaks
1/2 tsp almond essence

Put 200ml of the milk, the saffron water and seeds from 12 cardamom pods into a pan. Bring to the boil, remove from the heat and leave to infuse for half an hour. Beat the 230g sugar with the egg yolks, then pour the flavoured milk through a sieve into the egg mixture, discarding the seeds. Pour the mixture into a pan and gently heat, constantly stirring, until you have a thin custard; too much heat and the custard will curdle. Allow to cool, then refrigerate. Fold 600g of the yoghurt and the whipped cream into the custard and freeze until semi-frozen (about 8 hours), stirring twice while it's freezing. Warm the remaining 450ml of milk with the almond essence, 2 tbsp sugar and the remaining cardamom seeds. Leave to infuse, chill, then strain as before, discarding the seeds. Mix with the remaining yoghurt in a processor and whizz up. To serve, remove the ice-cream from the freezer and refrigerate for a good hour until it softens. Scoop balls of ice-cream into beakers and top up with the almond lassi.

Cardamom Hill rice

The Cardamom Hills are a huge tropical forest world in southern Indians Idduki district of Kerala. Ranks of outsized cretaceous-looking plants flourish in the shade of tall trees and in the raised altitude of the hills, to produce tiny green fruits. Keralans pods are superior to others, for they're harvested at the correct green, after the kringa stage, when all the immature white seeds are fully-fledged, fragrant and black. Cardamom makes this pilau rice drop-dead gorgeous.

1 tbsp vegetable oil
12 cardamom pods, bruised
6 cloves
2 large cinnamon sticks
4 dried bay leaves
500g basmati rice, washed and drained
salt

Heat the oil in a large heavy-based saucepan, then add the spices and heat for a few seconds, or until they waft fragrant and begin to make popping noises. Stir in the rice, then add about 700ml of water; you need enough to cover the rice by about 2cm (the distance between the tip of your index finger to its first joint, is − literally − a handy measure). Add a good shake of salt, bring to a boil and bubble for 2 minutes, then cover with a well-fitting lid, turn down the heat to very low, so there's barely a murmur, and cook for a further 7-8 minutes. Turn off the heat, leave for at least 10 minutes, then fluff through with a fork. Fluff through again when ready to serve.

Garam masala whitebait with lime, yoghurt and mint

If you're up for chilli heat, serve this dish with some raw green chilli to perk things up even more.

500g whitebait or other small fry
2 tsp ground garam masala
plain flour, for dusting
400g thick yoghurt
1 clove garlic, crushed
handful of mint leaves, finely chopped
vegetable oil, for deep-frying
1 red onion, finely sliced
2 limes, halved

Toss the fry in the salt, pepper and spice, then sprinkle with a little flour and turn to coat. Beat the yoghurt with the garlic, mint and a touch of salt, and leave on one side. Heat a deep pool of oil in a wok or deep-fat fryer and deep-fry the spiced fish until crisp − about 1 minute. To serve, lay the slices of red onion across a platter, squeeze with lime juice and pile the crispy fry on top. Squeeze with more lime juice. Dip each mouthful into little bowls of the garlic yoghurt.

Tandooried chicken

I'm giving you the psychedelic version – for true tandoor colour. Chicken tandoori just ain't the same without it.

8 free-range chicken drumsticks or thighs, or
  4 breasts, skinned
salt
2 lemons
4cm piece fresh root ginger, peeled
4 cloves garlic, crushed
2 thin green chillies, deseeded and chopped
2 tsp garam masala
1 tsp red food colouring mixed with 3 tsp yellow
  colouring
8 tbsp thick yoghurt
chunk of butter
1 red onion, finely sliced into rings
2 good handfuls of mint leaves

If using breasts, cut each into three. Slash the meat with about three cuts in each chunk, then pile into a dish, sprinkle with salt and squeeze over the juice of 1 lemon. Massage everything in. Grate over the ginger, add the garlic, chillies, and garam masala, and massage this in too. Next, brush the chicken with the food colouring, then tumble with 4 tbsp of the yoghurt. Cover and refrigerate overnight.

To roast, turn the oven to its highest setting, then remove the meat from its spiced yoghurt bath and discard the excess yoghurt. Lay the pieces of chicken across a baking sheet, giving them plenty of room, then, once your oven is at furnace level, zap the chicken in and roast for 20 minutes (if it's off the bone, 15 minutes). Rub the pieces with the butter about halfway through their time — a sort of rub-baste (saves melting and brushing it on). Squeeze the other lemon over the onion rings and lightly season. Pile the mint and dressed onion (tipping over any collected lemon juice) on to plates with the tandooried chicken, and add a big spoonful of yoghurt to each. Flatbreads required.

Keema fry with mint and flatbreads

Bademiya Seekh Kababs is a Mumbai street café, in a backstreet at the rear of India's most prestigous lux hotel, the Taj Mahal. The Taj's customers flock here of an evening to eat all things with flatbreads at wonky tables on a busy pavement, without fork or knife. It's worldwide known by those in the know, and Bombay moves in every night. Their keema fry is a roti-wrap-and-dunker's heaven. Bung in some pre-boiled new potatoes halfway through the cooking if you want. Rotis, naans, parathas or chapatis will be needed.

Roughly chop the onion, ginger, chillies and garlic, then blitz in a processor until very finely chopped, adding the ground cumin and coriander. Fry the mixture in the oil, with a little salt and pepper, until it starts to brown. Stir in the mince, breaking it up, season lightly again, and fry for a couple of minutes or so, or until browned a little. Pour in about 150ml water (or stock — a lamb or chicken stock cube is fine), cover, and gently bubble for 40 minutes. Chuck in the peas and garam masala, stir, then cook for another 5 minutes, adding extra water or stock if it needs it. Stir through half of the herb, then spoon the keema fry into a serving bowl, leaving any excess fat behind. Scatter with the onion bathed in lime juice. Bung on the remaining greenery and eat with oven-warmed flatbread.

1 medium onion
3cm piece fresh root ginger, peeled
2 green chillies
6 cloves garlic
2 tsp each ground cumin and coriander
4 tbsp vegetable oil
salt and pepper
400g lamb mince
big handful of podded peas
1 tsp ground garam masala
small bunch of mint or fresh
  coriander, roughly chopped
1/2 red onion, very finely sliced into
  rings, bathed in the juice of 1 lime

Juhu Beach bhel puri

Saturday night, and Bombay empties out on to Juhu Beach. Aunties, uncles, grans and nieces hold hands and enter the water, saris and all. There are pony rides through the surf; ferris wheels; dancing monkeys; street-wise kids touting knick-knacks, kites, balloons and snacks on the sand; barrows filled with hot coals and loaded with chilli-rubbed corn-cobs; and bhel puri wallahs aplenty handing over little stainless-steel plates of layered potato, crispy sev noodle, tomato and onion, drenched with tamarind and sweet chutney for a few rupees.

The unusuals in this can all be bought ready-made from Indian stores. (See right).

4 tbsp tamarind water (see page 236), or 2 tbsp lemon juice
2 tbsp sweet mango chutney
120g sev Bombay mix
12 bought crisp pooris, part crushed, or a handful of puffed rice (optional)
1 red onion, finely sliced
6 cooked new potatoes, roughly chopped
1 green (unripe) mango or 1/2 deseeded cucumber, shredded
2 tomatoes, sliced or chopped
stuffed handful of coriander leaves

Mix the tamarind with the mango chutney (if using lemon, add 2 tbsp water). Layer up all the ingredients on to plates, dressing each with the sweetened tamarind dressing as you go. May sound weird, yet tastes great.

Stove-grilled jumbo prawns with 20 garlic cloves

Little Indian about this. Just unadorned seafood, with the lift of garlic, curry leaves and butter. They dish up something similar for the tourists down by Cochin's Chinese fishing nets.

4 of the biggest shell-on prawns you can lay your hands on, or 4 lobster tails, uncooked and rinsed
salt and pepper
juice of 1 lemon
20 tiny cloves garlic, 3 peeled and crushed, the rest unpeeled
vegetable oil
1 sprig curry leaves, pulled from their stem
100g butter
lemon halves, to serve

Toss the prawns with plenty of salt and a twist of black pepper, the lemon juice and the crushed garlic, and leave on one side, covered, for about half an hour. Heat a heavy frying pan until medium hot, toss the whole garlic cloves in a dash of oil and some salt, then spread over the pan, cover and gently pan-roast until they're tender. Rub the prawns with 1 tbsp of oil and place them in the hot pan, tucking the resident garlic cloves around. Put a lid over the lot and roast away for about 3 minutes. Turn everything over, tuck in the curry leaves, and do the same for another 2-3 minutes. Remove from the heat, add the butter and turn through so everything is coated. Serve up with lemon halves to squeeze over and with finger bowls to rinse fingers.

Chilli salt and lime grilled corn-on-the-cob

A Juhu Beach easy.

100g butter, at room temperature
2 tsp crushed dried chilli or chilli flakes
salt and pepper
1/2 tsp freshly ground cumin
4 corn-cobs
1 lime, quartered

Mash the butter with the chilli, salt, pepper and cumin. Cook the cobs in boiling water for about 5 minutes then, when ready to grill, rub them with a little of the butter and grill over hot coals until they've taken on a bit of colour. Rub all over with the remaining butter and eat with squirts of lime.

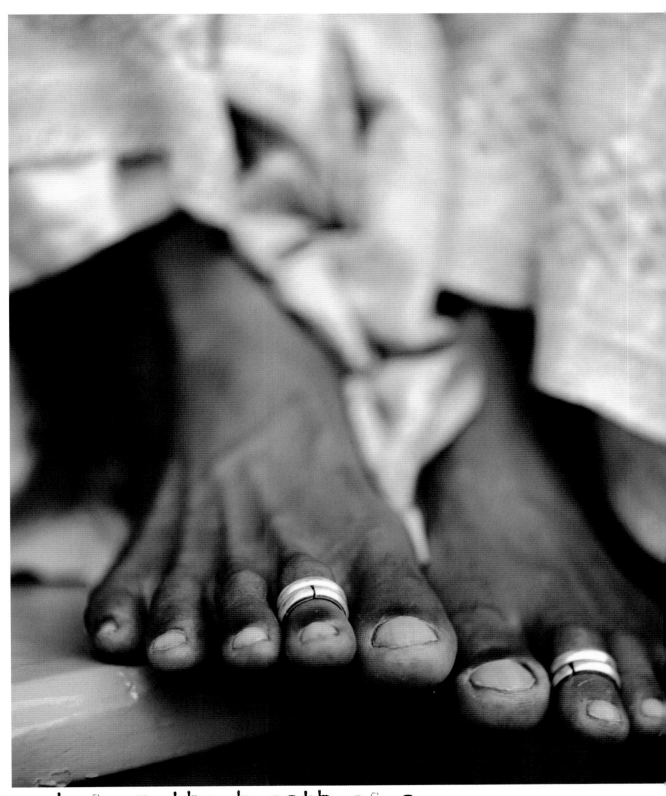

Apart from the breath of a
breeze catching the hem of her
sari, their slim fingers
skipping over the flutes are
the only things that move.

Saji's coconut sambar

Keralans would scoop this up with appams (rice pancakes). Use naan or other flatbreads instead, or eat with basmati rice. Other vegetables from beans and peas to bitter gourds, could be slung in too. Use what you have, what you know.

Grind the coriander, cumin and fenugreek seeds in a spice mill or coffee grinder. In a large wide saucepan, fry the onion, ginger and garlic in 2 tbsp oil until soft, then stir in the ground spices, chillies and turmeric and fry until golden. Add the vegetables and enough water to cover them, season, then leave to gently bubble until cooked through. Meanwhile, heat 2 tbsp of the oil in another pan and fry the mustard seeds and curry leaves for a few seconds and add them, with the oil, to the pot when the vegetables are almost cooked. Stir the coconut milk into the now reduced and heavily spiced water and bring to a gentle bubble, then add about 2 tbsp of the tamarind water. Taste and add more salt, pepper and tamarind to suit. Nestle the tomato quarters on top and leave to simmer for a further 2 minutes. The result should be velvety and soup-like.

2 tsp each coriander and cumin seeds
1 tsp fenugreek seeds
1 onion, finely chopped
3cm piece fresh root ginger, peeled and finely chopped
3 cloves garlic, sliced
vegetable oil, for frying
3 whole green chillies
1/4 tsp ground turmeric
800g vegetables (potatoes, carrots, peas, beans), scrubbed if necessary and thickly sliced
salt and pepper
2 tsp mustard seeds
2 sprigs curry leaves
1 x 400ml can coconut milk
2-3 tbsp tamarind water (see page 236), or 1 tbsp lemon juice
3 tomatoes, quartered

Curry leaf shrimp

Serve this dish with rice or naan breads, lime halves to squeeze over, and finger bowls to rinse fingers.

20 shell-on raw tiger prawns, heads removed
salt and pepper
1 narrow red chilli, deseeded and chopped
juice of 1 lime
12 small cloves garlic, 4 crushed
3 tbsp vegetable oil
2 tsp garam masala (preferably whole seeds)
2cm piece fresh root ginger, peeled and grated
2 sprigs curry leaves
1 onion, grated or finely chopped
5 plum tomatoes, roughly chopped
2 tbsp red onion or shallot slivers
1 red chilli, finely sliced
lime halves, to serve

Toss the prawns with salt and a twist of pepper, the chilli, lime juice and crushed garlic, and leave for half an hour. Heat a wide heavy frying pan until hot, and toss the prawns in 1 tbsp of oil, then sear them for about a minute on each side in the hot pan. Remove them from the pan. Add the whole garlic cloves and toss through, adding seasoning and a dash more oil if necessary. Cover and pan-roast on a low heat, shaking the pan occasionally, until fairly tender when tested with the tip of a knife. Turn the heat back up and add another tbsp of oil, the garam masala, ginger, curry leaves, onion and whole garlic cloves, turn and gently fry until you can smell the spices and the garlic has taken on a little of their colour. Return the prawns to the pan and turn so they pick up the spice. Add half the tomatoes and 2 tbsp water and cook for 5 minutes. Stir through the remaining tomatoes and the onion and chilli slivers, season again, and remove from the heat.

Prawn and mango curry

A fruitful number this. Some grated coconut (packet desiccated is fine too), fresh coriander leaves and little chunks of ripe mango can be served alongside. Poppadums wouldn't go amiss either. Look out for Alphonso mangoes, available from April to June. Slice into one of these blondes and you'll find thick, ochre-orange flesh that'll slip down, with a nectar and flavour as heady as it is bright. (See page 24).

5 cloves garlic, roughly chopped
3cm piece fresh root ginger, peeled and chopped
3 onions, roughly chopped
4 hot green or red chillies, left whole
6 cardamom pods, bruised
4 tbsp vegetable oil
2 sprigs curry leaves (optional)
3 tsp ground garam masala
2 tbsp Patak's Kashmiri Masala Paste
1 x 400g can chopped tinned plum tomatoes
1 x 400ml can coconut milk
2 large ripe mangoes (about 400g), peeled and cut
  into chunks
300g shelled raw tiger or other largeish prawns
salt

Put the garlic, ginger and onions in a processor and process to a paste, adding a drop of water if necessary. Fry the chillies and cardamom pods in the oil in a frying pan until the chillies blister, then throw in the curry leaves (if using) and fry for a further 20 seconds or so. Add the onion paste and 2 tsp of the garam masala and fry until the paste darkens in colour. Then stir through the Kashmiri Masala Paste — keep stirring to avoid burning. Add the plum tomatoes and 100ml water, and let everything bubble together for about 10 minutes. Stir through the coconut milk and the mangoes and bubble up for a further 10 minutes, adding an extra dash of water if it thickens too much. Stir in the prawns and cook for a further 3 minutes, or until the prawns are just cooked, stirring through the remaining garam masala and salt to taste just before serving. Serve in bowls, with rice, and shower with any bits and pieces you have.

Green chilli chicken

A quick and easy.

4 free-range chicken legs, jointed
  into thighs and drumsticks
vegetable oil
8 cloves garlic
3cm piece fresh root ginger, peeled
2 large onions
10 narrow green chillies, 4 chopped
2 tsp each ground cumin and coriander
1 tbsp paprika
1/2 tsp turmeric
salt and pepper
1 x 400g can peeled chopped tomatoes
2 tsp caster sugar

In a casserole pan, brown the chicken pieces on all sides in 3 tbsp oil until golden — do this in batches. Remove and leave on one side, leaving the oil in the pan. Roughly chop the garlic, ginger, onions and chopped chillies together, then put into a processor with a dash of water and pulverize to a paste. Mix in the spices, with some salt and an extra good twist of pepper. Fry this paste in the casserole, stirring often so that it doesn't catch, until it's well softened and browned. Stir in the tomatoes and sugar, bring to a bubble, and simmer for about 20 minutes. Put the browned chicken and whole chillies into the pan with enough water so that the meat is almost covered. Cover the pan, then place in a 180°C/350°F/Gas 4 oven and cook, stirring through once or twice, for about 40 minutes, until it is cooked through. It can now sit like this until you're ready — just reheat it in the oven or on the hob. Eat with naan breads or rice, yoghurt and fresh coriander.

Burma
flavours

Burma (Myanmar) is influenced by the same
neighbours as Vietnam, yet India is thrown into
the equation too, and so curries — but not as
we know them — play a strong hand in things.
There's the usual Asian flavour foursome of hot,
salty, sour and sweet. Yet there's nutty, tangy,
aromatic and bitter too. Buddhists are well
catered for because, as with Vietnam with its
long stretch of coast, seafood dominates and sea
and freshwater fish are sold live and restless
at every market. Curries are bolstered with
turmeric, pounded ginger and galangal, shallots
and garlic, and then fast-bubbled into peanut or
sesame oil-enriched sauces, containing little
spice, despite the affinity in name to their
equivalent in India. In fact, Burmese curries
are pretty tame and flounder in a fair whack of
oil, which is there to act primarily as a
preservative and is spooned off before eating.
The 'curry' nomenclature derives from the bits
and pieces — tangy pickles (pickled beansprouts
and radish tops) and citrussy leaves — that are
pulled, picked and spooned from plates and bowls
as you eat. A hot, bitter and clean soup will
be on board too. A crispy something, on the
puffed rice cracker front, is popular. Salty 'n'

crisp, such as deep-fried noodles, buffalo skin, shallot or dried prawns, will always accompany the clean-tasting and the fresh. As in all of Asia, ingredients are not thrown together in a hit-and-miss creative way; instead combinations have evolved through the physiological effects that they have on body and soul. For instance, tamarind leaf salad calms palpitations; tamarind sours soups to quench thirst, cool the stomach and fire up the appetite; and watercress soup with cumin leaves relieves asthma. Rice is the staple, along with wheat, egg and rice noodles (as used in mohinga, Burma's classic coconut-sauced fish noodles, and in shan pork noodles). And there's offal-led food, such as copper pot noodle soup (meatballs with liver and kidney). Pan-roasted chickpea flour is used to thicken noodles, beancurd dishes and papaya salads. Balachong is the country's salt and pepper: hot, tangy and shrimpily pungent, it's the life-blood of the Burmese table. It's a fried mulch-like paste of shallot, shrimp paste, dried shrimp, chilli flakes and garlic, sharpened with tamarind. Fermented shrimp paste, fish sauce, dried shrimp, dried salt-fish, and ripe tamarind pastes are all out there too. Lavish amounts of lemongrass, kaffir lime, coriander and other fragrant leaves are tossed with seafood dishes and curries, toasted peanuts are tossed with salads, and China has lent its seasoners of soy and oyster sauces. Pepper, cardamom, clove, cinnamon and fenugreek pop up, but coyly, here and there. A regular mix of white radish (mooli), wing beans, lettuces, vast chives and herbage, pumpkin, aubergines and tomatoes go to market every day, and there's cauliflower from the British days, which they appear to be mad for. Plus there's calabash gourd, chayote, pea tips, tree blooms, vegetable buds, stems, seeds and late-summer wild leaves and flowers. Green tea leaves are pressed and pickled, then mixed with toasted sesame seeds, split peas and fried garlic to make an after-dinner digestive – lepet, a delicious salad. And they're big on all things tempura-ed too. The unusuals are water beetles, some unattractive grubs, sambhur (antelope), and deep-fried fledgling (heads, feet and all). Eating out at tables happens chiefly at tea houses, which serve Thermos flasks of fragrant tea with a multicultural mix of dim sum buns, samosas and sticky almond stuffed pastries.

We stop for tea at
a dusty table

i climb dark narrow steps to where buddhas sit silent

From the land

5.30am. It's pitch black, I'm late, and the boat waits at the Ayeyerwady River for Bagan. I scramble out of a jeep, on to a steep bank and down a stairway lit by candles that flicker and flinch from the night-cool. Baskets of snacks and their sellers perch on steps that lead to water, moon-black and thick, where a hubbub of chat and music stirs boats. I clamber aboard, cutting it fine. A horn blows and we heave out, heavy, into a fug of blue smoke and blast; launching into the bitumen-black of night. The distant fires of the Mandalay shore dwindle, flicker, and are gone.

The ferry is carpeted with Burmese families in a shagpile of pots, pans, basketed things and bits, stacked and ordered as if ready to picnic, on rectangles of blanket and sack. Lower deck is steerage, sack and engine, where little faces peer out from blanket; the upper has a handful of flea-bitten cabins for a lie-down, if you dare, and the honk of root vegetable and spice steeps all. Dawn moves in and the river melts into a polish of stainless-steel shimmer, and our boat now sends ripples, silken and opal, to a shoreline of indefinite greys. The duskiest of pinks takes hold, splodged with the putty of cloud, and first-light silhouettes a palm-frayed horizon, lanced by spire. Then the fat old orb ascends, like a gong, as large, as orange and as flame, as a 1970s Athena poster sun. Its warmth prods at the outer wraps of those all huddled around, prompting a search in tiffin tins for rice and curries. I have my hotel picnic pack – a little box of great expectation, which is dashed by a cold boiled egg, dry croissant and a most unwelcome bottle of mineral water, so I look for my dawn chorus elsewhere.

Music starts. A tribal wood-on-wood beat, meandering, exotic, with a woman's sing-song, her camper high notes distorted as she ascends into the giddy heights of something distinctly Yma Sumac. The penetrable whiff of shrimp paste and balachong (a mix of fried shallot, chilli and dried shrimp) invades. Some perked, some provoked, people now shed blankets. The kitchen –

a mere coal grate, pans and a chopping board by a window (so that peel and stuff gets chucked out back) with two poly-bags of spice stuck on nails and some rat-proof chests – moves in on breakfast, and all goes up-beat. Now a male voice sings, there's a sitar and a pipe of kinds, all in the throes of a Bollywood spectacular. The wok cook turns chilli trigger-happy. Women with baskets of things work the travellers for their dollars and kyat. Catch the eye of a banana and biscuit seller, and they'll latch on, lock in and close in for the kill. As the hours pass by persistance increases, resistance decreases. Oh, go-on-then, gimme that banana.

A stop at Myanmu, halfway downriver, and gangplanks are thrown down, there's more green banana loading, and the samosa and watermelon girls pile on – to be herded off as we pull out again. Lunch is at our boat kitchen, at a long bench table: fried rice and vegetable pickles. With a chilli merchant whose teeth put me off my rice. A handful of French tourists join in on seeing that the table doesn't bite; while a German wanders about with a double-lens camera, a twin thing, scaring the living daylights out of those below deck.

Our next interlude is Semeikhon, where the bank heaves with bullock carts and stuff. Bad teeth exits, and more green bananas enter. The tourists gawp. The set stares back, waving goods at us. Our cameras click back. The boat's real full and heavy now, and the foreigners a little pink with all the unfamiliar. We shove off. The Ayeyerwady gurgles back into motion, and we slither ever onward into the unknown ahead. In truth, there's little to be seen between stops: a single dose of bank, tree, clump of trees, beast or shack is fed to us, like comfort food – without surprises – in an endless strip of sand and green. Sometimes it looks like Sussex, in a fieldy-pastoral-dotted-ancient-oak kind of way, then a palm or uhtaut (coned hat) changes everything. We chunter. I bask in sameness and thoughtlessness. Blankets get hung up as sunscreens. Below deck they've now built the Wall of

China in green bananas. The boat lop-sides, like a fat old carnival float. Preserved green tea leaves in sacks ballast out her other side, oozing tannin and treacly trickles across the teak deck. A refugee encampment of basket, person and blanket are jigsawed to fit, looking like one of those wallpaper-type puzzles that, when you screw your eyes up and look cross-eyed, is supposed to go all 3D and make sense. A would-be hippy sits in the annexe, on the way to the loo, holding court with any local careless enough to want the toilet. He talks to young Burmese girls, almost in their pants.

Afternoon ebbs and dark takes over. Seventeen hours is a long seventeen, and we pull in at Bagan's dock, 100 slow miles notched up, cold and aching for arrival and home. Our guide, U Law Win, meets us: as skinny as Ghandi, neat and smart in white matching linen ingyi and longyi (jerkin and sarong), his mouth reptilian with betel juice. He shoots words like machine-gun fire, and I want bed. Out there, somewhere in the dark, is the unsung wonder of an ancient world: the fallen kingdom of Bagan, dotted over 40 square kilometres of plain, all cradled in this last eight-mile sweep of the Ayeyerwady. Little travelled. Little known. One of the unique religious and architectural monuments of the world. I can't sleep – it's that Father Christmas feeling all over again.

Dawn. Swathes of sleepy mist dream about, like some Tales from the Crypt director has brought in all the dry-ice machinery he could muster – and just for me, for the full-theatre effect. A rolling plain of pinnacles, pagoda and edifice floats in a pooling cobweb of white: a sea of temples once built for serious worship, now looking like an abandoned filmset. Temples upon temples. Stupas upon stupas. A kingdom of soaring pinnacles, to the virtuous, to aspiration. Magnificently exotic. Magnificently eerie. Magnificently defiant. I'm magnificently moved. Built between 1057 and 1287, the 5,000 temples and stupas of Bagan eventually fell to the Mongols when Kublai Khan's archers brought Bagan's war elephants

of green ghosts

to their knees in the battle of Vochan. The myth of the invincible Elephas maximus army was shattered, the dark forces from the north took hold, and there was to be no return of the King. Yet 2,000 monuments are left standing today. Some are still crumbling, most restored – and all, well, out of this world. Marco Polo was the first traveller to clap eyes on the place in 1298, when it was still just clutching its heyday, and he spoke of temples of gold. And the fairytale reads on. The ruins became home to the goings-on of night: bandits, murderers and nats (ancient animistic spirits that are said to reside in Mount Popa, the 'Eye' on Bagan's far shadowy horizon). Yet the stiff upper-lip of British rule sent them all packing and, since the British have been ousted, spires have been re-gilded. Much work has been done since the earthquake of 1975 which saw many a sikhara (spire) topple. Another world put to rights by auntie UNESCO, so that future dawns and sunsets will forever keep this place something out of Once Long Ago.

A legend it may well become, for the Tatmadaw, Burma's notorious military rule, have stuck their hands into the restoration programme in a bare-faced attempt to legitimize their regime. To woo the tourist and his cash. Buddhist donors are being offered religious merit in return for sponsorship, and the fruits of their gifts are culminating in monuments being re-erected in an uncoordinated programme of regeneration: stupas are rising from the rubble, patched with modern brick, and built without accurate historical reference. It's great to see Bagan as a functional working Buddhist centre with an active social role in today's Burma and with an autonomy beyond tourist worship, yet such Disneyfication could lead to it losing its World Heritage Site rosette.

Morning rays now splice the mist, like one of those catastrophe old masters where God appears perched in the clouds, omnipotent and wielding deliverance. Night is sucked back into screaming black portholes, giving way to brightness and visitors of day, and

U Law Win takes me on a tour to show me the less obvious: wall paintings and frescoes, lost in the darkest and mouldiest of places, where strange little men with keys (and one with a tea-cosy hat) unlock the way to narrow passages and you look at something important yet murky on the walls. We temple around a bit with our driver who is quiet and smiling, handing out water and wipes, and then head for Bagan's 'Eye', Mount Popa.

Mount Popa is a get there, have lunch, exhaust yourself on yet more temple steps, and go home, thank-you-very-much, kind of a day. It lacks Bagan's mythical chemistry. But the temple is mad and worth the haul up, plus there are 37 nats in all their natty finery to be seen at the foot of the hill: human effigies in dressing-up-box garb, looking like 1950s seaside-style waxworks. That sort of affair. The temple clusters on top of a rocky outcrop with Gaudi-like baubling mirror mosaic hugging its ramparts, the gold ice-cream cones of stupa marking its perimeter. It's a stiff climb: vertiginous metal flights of stairs with evil little monkeys running riot on the way, as bad-tempered as their red-raw bums. On top are tiled shrines with the usual collection of glass tanks for money donations, as if someone is setting up an aquarium shop. Bananas and things heave at effigies' feet, and grim-faced wooden individuals – in lurid modeller's paint – are massed around beds, offerings, paintings and photos. Jake and Dinos Chapman material. 'Unusual', my mum would say.

On the descent, we rest at a food stall and sit on doll's-house-sized furniture to eat delicate plates of papaya salad made by a plump woman with a face as broad as a bullock cart. She squats stalwart, legs akimbo, a large tin platter of expertly lacerated green fruit and herb shreds piled like mini-mountain ranges at her side. One hand does dainty things, nimbly mixing and kneading; the other slings fists of stuff at the monkeys to keep them at bay. She pours and trickles things, as if preparing a libation for the gods. This gets woven with needles of kaffir lime leaf, bean paste, toasted

chickpea flour, and toasted peanut oil and tamarind spooned into the dressing. On the return we stop for tea at a dusty table; it comes with lepet, a dish of fresh tea leaves pickled and fried in garlic and chilli, plus fried dried beans, peanuts and sesame seeds; and a pretty girl breezes up and sells us custard apples.

The evening brings a horse-drawn jig out to Sulamani Phato. With its Sleeping Beauty towers, for me it's Bagan's crown at sunset. The tale of tales, a jewel, built in 1181. Down dust tracks, skirting sesame and corn field, succulent and scrub, we weave a route through the towers of silence that dot the way. Robbed of their treasures, yet once a south-east Asian mecca for monks and the hub of the Burmese empire, they stand senile and redundant, empty barrows on an epic stage where the cast of thousands has walked out. The wind chime crowns on spires tinkle, consumed by the corrosion of heat. Farmers herd in cows. White flanks tight on rib. Stretched hide on bone. I climb up through dark narrow steps to where buddhas sit silent in a small temple east side of Sulamani. No-one is home. Just the fluster of pigeon echoes in the vaults. Two owls pop up, spooked. One after the other. In turn we look at each other, each of us as startled as the next. They swoop off, dissolving into their land of green ghosts.

The heat of day hums in thick walls of brick, brittle grasses whisper on the bleach of breeze, and Sulamani stands mighty, its pyramidal tiers soaring like Sauron's Middle Earth towers. The mouths of its dark doors silent; needles and points lance heavenward, black. It's as if the undead ride out. Then a gong and a chant somewhere distant break the silence. The sun larvals into the boiling oil of day-end colour and curries the sky with reds. A woman passes below, a thatch of firewood on her head. Her arms, legs and longyi flow warm and careless. The last rays lap to her, and her small brown feet tread out the dust of another day ◼

Dawn moves in and the river melts

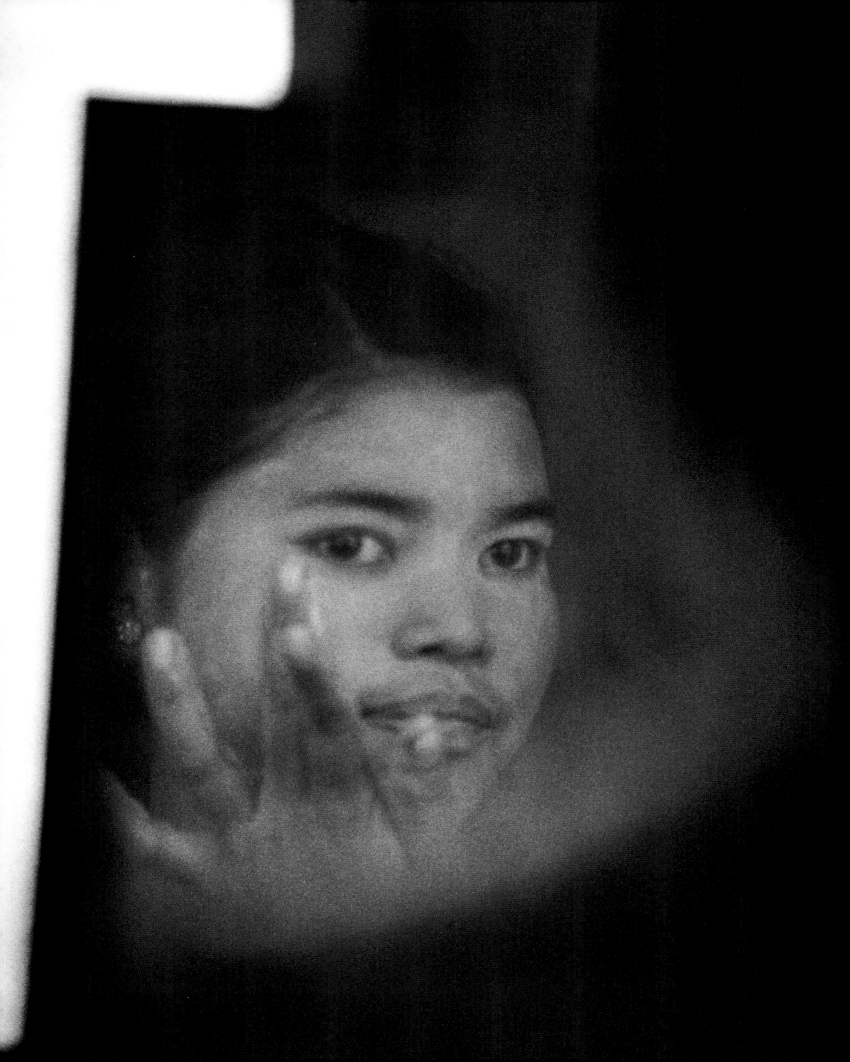

NGAPALI BEACH CHILLI CRAB, PAGE 74

The horizon twinkles like some
ghost promenade until dawn, and then
the boats are gone.

8.30am, I go to market - prime time, for by 11am it's ransacked and sad. Produce is hoovered up in a frantic push-and-shove of shopping basket, hand and banter. Plum-sized aubergines are weighed out, to jumble next to a fish or a bound crab; white radishes are piled like stupas; fat green truncheons of kalabash gourd with white marrow flesh are grabbed like they're going-out-of-fashion; freshly made rice vermicelli is bundled into banana leaf. There's much weighing out of flower heads, pinky-crimson umbels of pan chey puit (flowerbuds with a sour taste to add fragrance to clear broths); petals, the ochre-yellow of bird's foot trefoil and bitter herbs, shin bau, used in soups. The milk of scraped coconut pools in the cool areas, under propped umbrellas, between pockets of unshaded heat. There's sweet rice flour puddings baled and shaggy in shredded coconut and various coconut porridge puddings; sago and little worms of rice noodle – like spätzle or Italian strozzapreti – are topped with grated coconut, drenched with unfermented palm juice and made sweet and molasses-rich with jaggery. I buy a half-dozen bamboo-leaf-wrapped sticky rice parcels from a woman who wears the look of her labour of love. Her eyes and hand movements say her's to be just-the-job: wrapped,

bound and steamed, as neat as the tight bun of hair that sits trussed by a comb on the back of her head.

Breakfast here is rice vermicelli, and good. Food stalls sell it tossed with snipped lengths of fried tofu, coriander, peanut oil and balachong (a thick, deep beetle-red, coarse paste, a fibrous mulch of fried pounded dried shrimp, shallot, garlic, chilli flakes and tamarind). I sit on a bench at a Fablon-covered table while my vermicelli lady pops about like a myna bird, eyes raven black and nimble on her perch. Her head cocked this way and that, dutifully responding to my pointing as she pecks at things with her fingers, like a bird would at pots in its cage. She then passes me a glorious nest of the stuff and a bowl of sharp broth to make it swim. A little tune of thanks and some more bobbing up-and-down are my goodbye ∎

A beast of a thing blows in that evening. A whirring, bristling ship of the night. As big as a bird. Undercarriage lowered, wheels down, wings in reverse thrust, it crash-lands on the floorboards of Moe Cherry's restaurant with a thump and angry crumpled buzz. A bug, a beetle, so big as to have a voice. Tropically large, and tropically noisy. Of the sort that made my encyclopaedia thrilling as a child; the one I'd scare my sister with, just by showing her the picture. Pinned on a board in the Science Museum it would make us all tingle, yet here it's live and, more worryingly, clumsily mobile. So now I'm on my feet. Moe's feeding travellers with curries, rice and beers – travellers who have flocked to her friendly verandaed first floor in Mrauk U. She now slops over, curvaceous, in her flip-flops – her gold mules kicked off at the bottom of the stairs. So confidently big is this bug that it doesn't budge when Moe comes to sort it out. She pulls at one of its foot-long whiskers, and it nods, like one of those car back-window dogs, emitting a loud grumpy cackle, a critter-like snigger, and doesn't budge. Wings now precision stowed, it's a fine-tuned piece of jungle engineering. Its beige carapace is blotched with red and beautifully crafted. Moe says it's their nan yone kung, their June bug, as that's when they're everywhere and on the mate. We all give it a hesitant prod to hear more cackle, and then she lovingly lets it crawl up her pink cardi-sleeve ∎

Mrauk U market

Nan Yone Kung

Green tomato salad

Firm under-ripe red tomatoes could be used
instead of green. (See left).

1 clove garlic, crushed
1 tbsp caster sugar
2 1/2 tbsp lime juice, plus 1/2 tsp
   finely grated zest
1 tbsp fish sauce
4 green tomatoes, cut into wedges
4 pink shallots or 1 small red onion,
   finely sliced
4 tiny red or green chillies, sliced
3 kaffir lime leaves, very finely
   shredded, or a handful of chopped
   fresh coriander
peanut (groundnut) oil
3 tbsp toasted crushed peanuts (see
   page 236)

Mix the garlic with the sugar, lime juice, zest and
fish sauce until the sugar has dissolved, then toss
through the tomatoes, shallots, chillies and shredded
lime leaves or chopped coriander. Leave to sit for
20 minutes or so, then serve, splashed with a little
peanut oil and drenched with peanuts.

Pickled beansprouts

1 tsp salt
100ml rice vinegar
250g beansprouts

Stir the salt with
the vinegar and 300ml
water in a saucepan,
and bring to the
boil. Pour over the
beansprouts and
leave to cool. Best
eaten straightaway,
but will keep for
two days, covered and
refrigerated. Drain
before eating.

Mount Popa green papaya salad

Papaya salad is to Asia what spag bol is to the West: adored, loved, eaten at every opportunity and in countless
variations – each to his own. Here's one glorious variation.

2-3 tbsp chickpea (gram) flour
2 tbsp peanut oil
2 shallots, finely sliced
2 cloves garlic, finely sliced
150g beancurd, cut into thin strips
1 green papaya, peeled, deseeded and
   finely shredded
4 kaffir lime leaves, finely shredded
handful of roughly chopped fresh
   coriander leaf and stem
2 tbsp lemon or lime juice (or
   tamarind water, see page 236)
2-3 tsp caster sugar
1 tbsp fish sauce
1-2 tsp chilli flakes

Toast the chickpea flour in a hot, dry frying pan
until nutty brown all over – keep shaking the pan
so that it doesn't catch and burn. Heat the oil
with the shallots and slow-fry until the shallots
start to become crisp. Chuck in the garlic, fry
for a touch longer, then remove from the heat and
leave to cool. Toss the flour and the onion and
garlic oil with the beancurd and papaya, then
toss in all the remaining ingredients and work
well together. Give it a taste, then add more of
whatever you may feel it yearns. Hot, salty,
sour, sweet and fragrant it should be – with
crunch and slither.

OCTOPUS, CHILLI AND
HERB SALAD, PAGE 64

Railway station chicken

Eaten in, and therefore christened after, Yangon railway station. Old Rangoon's terminus to Empire. Our chick was much more exuberant than the weary tables and cloths of the station's forecourt restaurant had led us to expect. (See right).

2 cloves garlic, crushed
3cm piece fresh root ginger, peeled
  and finely shredded
2 red birdseye chillies, finely sliced
2 tbsp caster sugar
5 tbsp lime juice
3 tbsp fish sauce
2 large free-range chicken breasts,
  skinned
salt and pepper
groundnut or vegetable oil
a small bunch of fresh coriander

For the dipping sauce, mix together the first six ingredients and stir until the sugar has fully dissolved. Cut the chicken breasts into small chunks, then tumble with a little salt and pepper and 1 tbsp of the dipping sauce, cover, and leave to bathe for about 30 minutes. Heat a shallow pool of oil in a wok, then fry the chicken nuggets in two batches for 3-4 minutes, or until cooked through, draining each lot on kitchen roll. Serve around the bowl of dipping sauce, lavished with coriander.

Octopus, chilli and herb salad

Octopus, fresh from the Bay of Bengal; shredded blades of saw-tooth coriander, fresh from Thandwe market; all jumbled with lime juice, salt, chilli and onions... need I say more? You'll find it all at home too. (See page 62).

Bring a pan of salted water to a rolling boil, then pop in the whole octopus and gently simmer for 30-40 minutes, depending on size, or until just tender (test with a knife). Next, drain, slice off and discard the head and beak (located in the ring-hole of the tentacles), then slice the ring of tentacles into arms and cut these into sections. Warm the peanut oil and garlic until the garlic starts to turn golden, then remove from the heat. In a large bowl, mix the sugar with the lime juice, shredded lime leaves or zest and fish sauce until the sugar has dissolved, then toss through the sliced octopus, with the tomatoes, shallots, chillies and garlic-infused peanut oil. Cover and leave to sit for about 20 minutes or so, taste and add a touch of salt if it needs it. Tumble through the coriander just before serving.

1 medium octopus, thoroughly rinsed
2 tbsp peanut oil
2 cloves garlic, finely chopped
1 tbsp caster sugar
2 1/2 tbsp lime juice
3 kaffir lime leaves, very finely
  shredded, or 1/2 tsp finely grated
  lime zest
1 tbsp fish sauce
4 firm tomatoes, cut into slim wedges
  and deseeded
4 pink shallots or 1 small red onion,
  finely sliced
4 tiny hot red chillies, finely sliced
salt
handful of long coriander (saw-tooth
  herb) or regular coriander leaves

Inle Lake lamb curry

Heavenly lamb dumplings in a punchy tomato sauce – sort of mum's meatballs go comfortably into Asia. I scoffed it daily on Inle Lake: a vast tract of water that supports various villages around its shores – on land, and on stilts, complete with floating gardens. The villagers lead the Life of Pi, on the water with their livestock. Fish plop, dragonflies hum, and insects buzz all day long around waters dappled with Hockney squiggles and abstractions aplenty. The place of escape. Mick Jagger was here one week before I visited – furious when at last somebody recognized him. (See left).

1 onion, chopped
4cm piece fresh root ginger, peeled and
  sliced
3 cloves garlic, chopped
2 sticks lemongrass, trimmed and chopped
500g lamb mince
2 fresh red chillies, deseeded
a bunch of fresh coriander
salt
2 tbsp fish sauce
2 tsp cornflour
peanut oil
2 tsp each of paprika and dried chilli
  flakes
1 tbsp dried shrimp, chopped, or 1 tsp
  shrimp paste
1 x 400ml can chopped tomatoes
3 tbsp tamarind water (see page 236),
  or 2 tbsp lemon juice and 1 tbsp
  water

Blitz the onion, ginger, garlic and lemongrass to a pasty mush in a processor or, if feeling energetic and in ethnic mode, pulverize in a mortar. Break up the mince in a bowl then squeeze the onion paste over the bowl, so that some of its juice trickles out and into the meat. Keep the onion paste on one side. Finely chop the chillies and about half of the coriander – this can be done in the processor too – and toss with the meat. Then chuck in 1 tsp salt, 1 tbsp fish sauce and the cornflour and tumble again. Form into walnut-sized balls, then chill until firmed. Fry the meatballs in 3 tbsp of oil until browned all over, then leave to drain.

Meanwhile, gently fry the paprika powder, dried chilli flakes and shrimp in the same oil, until the oil reddens a little. Slip in the pulverised onion paste with a sprinkling of salt and fry until browned. Tip in the chopped tomatoes, then fill up the empty can with water and put it by the stove. Add the tamarind water and the remaining 1 tbsp fish sauce to the pan, stir through and bubble up to a splutter, then turn down the heat and let it gently rumble for about 20 minutes or so, stirring occasionally. Add the water from the can in dribs and drabs as things start to thicken, and season again. It should end up dark and rich looking – a bit like a chilli con carne, yet darker. Then pop in the meatballs, dunking them under, and cook at a gentle pace for a further 10 minutes or so. If things start to look dry, add a dash of water. Serve awash with chopped coriander, and with rice on the side. Table pickles, and a little wheel of veg and herb on a platter could come into play too here.

Mandalay Hill noodles

A novel in hand and a bag of market-bought noodles to fuel my adventure, chunter down the Kaladan River from Mrauk U toward Sittwee. It's the African Queen revisited, and a slurryous gurgle comes from her loins. Full-on stuff. As are the glorious noodles. Use sliced fish cake, chicken, pork or prawns in here, if you prefer to be more affluent about it. A little bowl of spring-onion-flavoured chicken broth on the side would be ideal. Balachong (see below) is a must. (See left).

groundnut or peanut oil
2 cloves garlic, finely chopped
250g tofu
salt
4-5 tbsp chickpea (gram) flour or
  plain flour, toasted in a dry hot pan
  until lightly browned
300g rice vermicelli noodles, cooked
  according to the packet's instructions
medium bunch of fresh coriander, stems
  and leaves chopped
1 tbsp tamarind water (see page 236)
  or lemon juice
2 tbsp Balachong (see below)

Heat 2 tbsp of the oil and slow-fry the garlic until it starts to turn gold. Remove from the heat and leave the oil to infuse and get really garlicky. Slice the tofu into thick strips. If your tofu has come floating in whey, it will have to be drained on plenty of kitchen roll for an hour or so. Dust the strips with salt and roll in 3 tbsp of the toasted flour, then gently fry in the groundnut or peanut oil until golden (I slip them into a pool of oil in a wok). Scissor the tofu into thinner strips once cool. Toss the noodles with the garlic oil, tofu strips, 1-2 tbsp of the toasted chickpea flour, coriander, tamarind and Balachong until well slicked in everything, and serve. Great picnic food: poly-bag up portions, with disposable chopsticks.

Pickled radish and greens

1 tsp salt
100ml rice vinegar
5cm piece large radish (preferably
  white radish, mooli/daikon), sliced
200g sliced sharp greens (radish
  tops, cabbage, anything brassica
  and green)

Stir the salt with the vinegar and 300ml water in a saucepan and bring to the boil. Pour over the radish and greens and leave to cool. Best eaten straightaway, but will keep for two days, covered and refrigerated.

Balachong

Balachong is the raunchiest 'salt and pepper' I've had the pleasure of. Hot, tangy and shrimpily pungent. And it's the life blood of the Burmese table. If you want it to sing higher, add a little shrimp paste when you wok.

50g dried shrimp
4 shallots, finely sliced
4 tbsp peanut oil
2 tbsp crushed dried red chilli
4 cloves garlic, sliced
1 tbsp tamarind water (see page 236), or 1/2 tbsp
  lemon juice and 1/2 tbsp water

Briefly process the shrimp until they're coarsely crushed, or pulverize in a mortar. Slow-fry the shallots in the oil until they start to go brown and crisp, then scoop out excess oil and chuck in the dried chilli, shrimp and garlic and stir-fry until it all picks up some colour. Add the tamarind water or diluted lemon juice, then stir-fry for about 2 minutes, or until the mixture dries up - but don't let it burn. It should end up as a dark, damp coarse paste - peat-like.

Night fisherman's soup

The boats go out at night from Ngapali Beach to snare squid, prawns and tiny fish by light bulb and net. The horizon twinkles like some ghost promenade until dawn, and then the boats are gone – back to the village up by the creek. The catch ends up at the market, alongside the baskets of veg. This is one-pot cooking, and an easy, delicious, comforting end for a squid. (See right).

1 onion, chopped
4 cloves garlic, sliced
2 sticks lemongrass, trimmed and smashed
2 chillies, split and deseeded
2 tbsp fish sauce
2 tbsp lemon juice or 3 tbsp tamarind
  water (see page 236)
2 tsp caster sugar
salt
250g mixed chopped vegetables, such as
  cauliflower, Chinese greens, carrot,
  green beans, calabash gourd or
  chayote
250g fresh shelled prawns
250g prepared and skinned squid tubes,
  cut into rings
2 tomatoes, roughly chopped
handful of shredded long coriander
  (saw-tooth herb) or regular
  coriander leaves

Put the onion, garlic, lemongrass, chillies, fish sauce, lemon juice and sugar with 1.5 litres water and a sprinkling of salt in a large saucepan. Bring to a bubble and gently simmer for about 10 minutes. Add all the prepared vegetables, making sure they're cut to a size that will allow them to cook through at the same time. Once they're almost tender – about 5 minutes – add the prawns and squid and cook for a further 2 minutes. Stir in the tomatoes and taste, adding a dash more salt if it needs it. Remove, discard the lemongrass and serve lavished with shredded coriander.

Best friend squid salad

Some nice ladies with polite lanterns at the Best Friend restaurant, Ngapali Beach, tumble this punchy salad together nightly.

500g prepared and skinned baby squid tubes
1 clove garlic, crushed
1 tbsp caster sugar
2 1/2 tbsp lime juice, plus 1/2 tsp finely grated zest
1 tbsp fish sauce
4 firm tomatoes, cut into slim wedges and deseeded
4 pink shallots or 1 small red onion, finely sliced
4 tiny hot red chillies, finely sliced
1/2 tsp salt
3-4 tbsp toasted crushed peanuts (see page 236)

Boil the squid in water to cover for 2 minutes, then drain and leave to cool. In a large bowl, mix the garlic with the sugar, lime juice, zest and fish sauce until the sugar has dissolved, then toss through the cooked squid, tomatoes, shallots, chillies and salt. Cover and leave to sit for about 20 minutes or so, then pile on to a platter or plates and serve drenched with the toasted crushed peanut.

Ngapali Beach chilli crab

White-fleshed crab is wanted here, but if you're in the wrong place for such tropical water delicacies (blue swimmer crabs or mud crabs, say), use nice fat whole claws instead. I scoffed this nightly on Ngapali Beach, far away in time. Gorgeous. (See page 55).

4 uncooked tropical water crabs, or 8 big cooked
  crab claws
3cm piece fresh root ginger, peeled and chopped
3 cloves garlic
6 small shallots, chopped
2 tsp each dried chilli flakes and paprika
1 tsp dried shrimp or 1 tbsp fish sauce
3-4 tbsp peanut oil
1/2 tsp shrimp paste
1/4 tsp ground turmeric
salt
4 tomatoes, skinned and chopped
8 small green or red chillies, left whole
4 kaffir lime leaves

Ask your fishmonger to split the crabs into quarters, and to lightly bash the claws to crack their shells, yet leave the shell intact and on the meat (easily done with a rolling pin at home). In a processor, blast the ginger, garlic and shallots to make a coarse paste. Gently fry the dried chilli flakes, paprika and dried shrimp in the oil until the oil reddens a little. Stir-fry the crabs in two batches in the flavoured oil until seared and reddened all over. Scoop them out, leaving the oil behind, then slip in the pulverized onion paste with the shrimp paste, turmeric and a sprinkling of salt, and fry until it looks reddened. Stir in the tomatoes, chillies, lime leaves and a touch more salt (if needed) and bubble up, adding a dash of water. Rapidly cook for 10 minutes, adding more water if necessary. It should end up paste-like, rich and unctuous. Slip the crab back in and cook in the paste, stir-frying, for 5 minutes or so, until the crab is cooked. Eat with rice, finger bowls ready.

Hill station chicken curry with new potatoes

A shivery night at Maymyo Hill Station was rescued by this curry. The only welcome thing to be seen or had. Curry adornment at the table is essential in Burma – herbage, pickled or blanched veg and boiled eggs are the possibilities to be toying with here. A colonial favourite, sure of it.

salt and pepper
4 skinned free-range chicken breasts,
  cut into chunks
3 tbsp groundnut or vegetable oil
1 tsp chilli flakes
3 tsp paprika
1 large onion, chopped
3cm piece fresh root ginger, chopped
4 cloves garlic, chopped
1/2 tsp ground turmeric
1 tbsp fish sauce
400ml Asian chicken stock (see page 236)
800ml coconut cream
8 cooked baby new potatoes

To serve
handful of chopped shallots and fresh
  coriander
pickled beansprouts (optional, page 61)

Salt and pepper the chicken chunks, then briefly fry in the oil until lightly browned all over. Remove the chicken, then add the chilli flakes and paprika to the oil and heat gently for about a minute before turning off the heat. This will redden the oil. Blast the onion, ginger and garlic in a processor to a coarse paste. Spoon the paste into the pan of chilli oil, along with the turmeric, and fry for about a minute. Next, tip in the browned chicken and the fish sauce, stir through and continue to fry for about 3 minutes. Pour in the stock, stir through and bubble up, then gently cook for about 10 minutes, stirring occasionally to prevent sticking. Stir in the coconut cream and the potatoes and gently cook for a further 10 minutes, until the chicken is cooked through. Serve with rice, and with pickled bits and pieces to fling on top.

Green ginger river prawn curry

We pull in from the Lay Myo River and lunch at a sun-bleached stilted shack, under which hoglets and puppies rootle and flop about. Fish, kippered to bloaters, slashed and threaded on bamboo sticks, are gently warmed over a fire, and taste of delicious hut. Fat river prawns, as big as lobster tails, are fried with smashed green ginger and salt, then plopped into a bubbler of a curry. Heads are sucked of their glories by those who know – and are happy to do. So, keep the prawn heads on, but snip off the ends (all the whiskery bits), so the goodness works into the curry.

12 extra large uncooked prawns in shell
1 tbsp fish sauce
8 kaffir lime leaves, 4 finely shredded
5cm green (young) root or fresh root
   ginger, peeled and grated
5 tbsp peanut or groundnut oil
3 tsp paprika
1 dried chilli, crushed, or 1 tsp
   chilli flakes
1 red chilli, deseeded and finely chopped
1 tsp shrimp paste (preferably
   toasted), or 1 tbsp fish sauce
3 cloves garlic
6 small shallots, chopped
1/4 tsp ground turmeric
5 tomatoes, skinned and chopped
salt

Peel the prawns, leaving on the heads and tail bits – and keep the shells. Slit the backs of the prawns, pull out the dark tract and chuck it. This is not necessary on smaller prawns. Toss the prawns with the fish sauce and a shredded lime leaf, and tip over any collected ginger juice from the grated ginger. Toss through, cover, and leave on one side. Crush the shells up a bit – in a mortar or with a knife. In a frying pan or wok, gently heat the oil with the paprika, chilli flakes and chilli, and allow to stew for a few minutes, or until the oil has developed a good red colour, then chuck in the shells and gently fry for about 5 minutes. Sieve the flavoured oil into a wok, discarding all the bits and pieces.

Pound together the shrimp paste, ginger, garlic, shallots and turmeric to make a coarse paste – or blast together in a processor. Fry the paste in the flavoured oil until softened and lightly browned, then stir in the prawns and fry these too for about a minute. Lift out the prawns, leaving the paste in the wok, and keep on a plate on one side. Stir in the chopped tomatoes, whole lime leaves and a touch of salt (if it needs it), and bubble up, adding a dash of water. Rapidly cook, with a bit of a splutter, for about 10 minutes – adding more water if things start to look at all dry. It should end up paste-like, rich and unctuous. Tip in the prawns with any collected juices, bed down in the sauce and gently cook for about 8 minutes or so. You may want to scoop off excess oil. Serve scattered with the remaining shredded lime leaves, and eat with rice.

Shan noodles

A bowl of green leaf soup or light broth sat alongside would be welcome – but only if you've got your authentic hat on. Bung something pickled in the veg department on top.

400g fresh wheat noodles (300g dried)
3 shallots, chopped
2cm piece fresh galangal or root ginger, peeled
2 cloves garlic
salt
peanut or vegetable oil
250g pork fillet, thinly sliced
1 tbsp fish sauce
2 tsp caster sugar
2 spring onions, chopped
small handful of chopped fresh coriander
1 tsp dried chilli flakes

Cook the noodles according to the packet, then drain, tossing them a little. Pound together the shallots, galangal and garlic with a good pinch of salt to make a paste. Fry the paste in 1 tbsp oil until softened, then toss through the pork, fish sauce and sugar. Stir-fry for 2-3 minutes or so, or until cooked and a little caramelized, then toss through the spring onions and noodles and remove from the heat. Fold through the coriander and chilli flakes. Pile into bowls and serve each bowl with 1 tbsp pork scratchings, anoint with a spoonful of pickled veg and put a bowl of green leaf soup alongside (if doing).

Thailand

Thai
flavours

Salty, hot, sour, bitter, fragrant, sweet, and all tossed together, that's how a Thai loves food. Punchy flavours and aromatics driven by fish sauce, dried shrimp, fiery chilli, lime juice or tamarind, lemongrass, galangal, ginger and herbs. These are tempered by the bland (rice); the toasted and crunchy (peanuts and fried shallots or garlic); the slippery (rice or glass noodles); the creamy (coconut milk); and the crisp (an array of fragrant leaves). Many Thais are of Chinese extraction, which explains the dichotomy of Chinese dishes with Thai dishes. At the table, seasoning comes as a dish of phrik nam pla (chillies in fish sauce) or another nam pla-seasoned dipping sauce. Thai food would be nowhere without nam pla. It's a must-have. Once upon a time, the West thought it stunk something rotten, but now we love it. It's made from plaa ka tak, a particular anchovy fished out of the emerald-blue waters of the Gulf of Thailand. Shrimp paste is another favourite. The Gulf, Indian Ocean, and Andaman Sea are Thailand's seafood shopping baskets, and beautiful things, vast catches, crustacea sweet and fresh, reach Thai markets daily. A feast.

The hours before

Banana and palm and unknown
exotics

COMFORT NOODLE SOUP, PAGE 99

I went to

It's hot, it's steamy, and it's exhaustingly busy. Bowls of this and woks of that fly, dip, flip and duck. Wide-line noodles and deep pans of steaming stock glint. Lipstick flashes of chopped chilli spin from boards into bowls, and the salt of nam pla (fish sauce) steeps the shadows. Saucing, dipping and spooning, shoppers eat, satiating tongues and convalescing swollen feet. I park-up, too, and sweat over a bowl of soup noodle bobbing with fish ball. Phew, it's hot, but deliciously so.

Chatujak, Bangkok's biggest market, has opened its gates to yet another frantic weekend of buy, sell and scoff – to the heart's content. Its core is a sauna of teenagers in denim, Gucci fake and flimsy T-shirt club gear, while its outer layers sell homewares, from the urban tasteful – palmwood bowl minimalism – to 2-baht kitchen plastic. At its perimeter, the bowl-food stalls full-steam it under a venting rag-tag of canopies. Its vast maze of alleys would take days to cover, yet meltdown for me is near. I beat a trail from its throbbing caldera, carried by the lava of cram, sweat and jostle, and am propelled out, ejected into flower-scented daylight.

Here, tinkling water cools a jungly periphérique. Waterlilied calm. A green fringe stuffed with herbage for gardens: buckets of soft pink-and-blue waterlilies, roses wrapped in banana leaves, orchids, fish and other exotics. Above, the rafters dangle with ornamental garden knick-knacks. Well turned-out veg and pets can be found around the corner, across a quadruple-laned, waltzing tuk-tuk crazed street.

Here hawkers sell locusts, bugs and grubs grilled and roasted to carapace-caramel-crisp perfection. Thais snack all day and I've caught the bug (if not quite for arthropoda) and opt for, from the back of a bike, khao larm: a charcoal-grilled baton of bamboo, stuffed to its joints with black bean coconut sticky rice and plugged, naturally, with a folded bamboo leaf. My kinda grub.

Here too are fat mangoes, papaya, maprang (an apricot-like fruit) and watermelon, much cut into geometric shapes, stuffed into inflated poly bags. Sliced green mango is bagged with a palm-sugar-sweetened shrimp dipping sauce, and roll-and-fold-your-own cha phlu leaves are bagged with toasted coconut and peanuts, shredded galangal, chips of lime peel and a fantastic caramelized sticky goo. All is rubber-banded, pert and fresh. Even my bottle of Coke is up-turned into a bag filled with ice, elastic-banded and stuck with a straw.

Back in town, it's jetty time for me at the Chang Pier, which leads on to the Chao Phraya River (next to the palace gardens). Here hawkers set up in the calm of a breeze under trees soporific with frangipane scent. Steam idles in drifts and oil muffles battered morsels that hit well-tuned pans. The cooking pace is ordered. Everything is in its rightful pot or stack. From a glass cabinet I choose white-cut chicken on fragrant rice with slices of cucumber and a stash of coriander. It comes on a pink plastic plate, with a bowl of nam jim kai (a dipping sauce of chilli flakes, soy bean paste and rice vinegar), an

accompanying cup of deliciously sweet chicken broth for further saucing, and an iced lemon-slush to drink. Then from another stall, I finish with a take-away snack: glass noodles bagged with white fungus, a feathery green leaf (pak ka chad) and crispy crumbled rice cake, all tossed with dribbles and splashes that pack in layers and punch.

Around the corner, in Sanam Luang Park, sound systems compete, and thousands of cobra kites dance the Bangkok sky, tails buckling and kinking. Where there's a gathering there's food, and meals-on-wheels weave through families picnicking on the turf. Eggs are grilled in the shell; wind-dried squid, as flat as book-marks, are clipped on threads, washing-line neat; women shovel blue-green mussels and clams into bags; and a cross-poled basket hawker pounds galangal, garlic and chilli with sugar in a mortar and passes up plates hay-stacked with som tam thai (green papaya salad). My day rounds off with khamom krog – dinky custard-cakes of coconut milk, rice starch and spring onion, baked in griddle cups. 'Welcome to the kingdom of Thailand,' my arrival card had said. Just a day of Bangkok's markets bestows gallons of that ∎

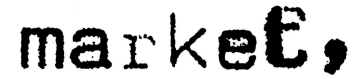

market,

Idling on, the night bloom of something

GLASS NOODLE SPRING ROLLS WITH NAM JIM, PAGE 98

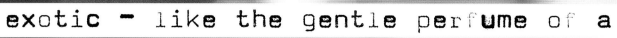

exotic - like the gentle perfume of a

great aunt

Carved fruit, macraméd loo roll and courtesy chocs on pillows you won't get. Bed is a mattress on the floor and en suite means a mere basin and tap. There's no pool, room service, MTV or air-con either. Swimming is a canal, music is bug buzz and the ambient temperature is a steamy-hot degrees C. There is only one way to taste Thailand. And, for me, this is it. Without garnish. In a ban song Thai – a traditional Thai house. The perfect antidote to the suffocating anaesthetic of corporate hotels. Hotel, motel, Holiday Inn? No thanks. I'll take a hut – and in the jungle, please.

So, with Bangkok's temples to power-shower luxury waved goodbye, I speed out south-west in a taxi, leaving its diesel-blown flyovers to heave, and move on into a richer kingdom that is Thailand. An hour and a half later, I'm deep in green, in the province of Samut Songkhram. Its lushness beams at me from everywhere. Banana and palm and unknown exotics forest a land of little wooden houses on stilts set among waterways (khlongs) that ebb, flush and flow with the adjacent Gulf of Thailand. We pull off the road and go through a small village with a humpback bridge and a fancy gabled temple. After passing some monks' quarters, we pull up in a lane of shadowy coconut palm where, deep between the coir trunks, is a hamlet of wooden homes.

The houses are reached on foot, by a series of paths, stepping stones and gangplanks over ditches and a khlong. A plop – and a toad legs it. Insects hum and buzz, rub legs and swap wheezes. A few squawks and whoops later, and I'm in a grassy yard of feather-duster-tailed chickens and old grans, their welcoming smiles stuffed with bad teeth. It's hot, yet the old women totter around as cool as cucumbers while I'm stuck to shirt and shorts. It's as if someone's closed the door on me and pressed boil-wash.

Far side, two old stilt houses stand with slopey roofs made of dark planks. Inside, they're generous and broody, with polished floors as glossy as chocolate ganache. In one, a black-and-white photo is the only wall decoration, apart from two glass-fronted cabinets, one stacked with blankets and clothes, the other with teapots and faded plastic blooms. A fan whirrs but fails to move the heat, and Mr Boonpud, my host, points out my bed – a mattress in one corner with a mosquito net. There's a verandah and a little jetty khlong-side, its eaves hung with orchid plants, like we'd basket-up busy lizzies or geraniums. And over a stream, there's a communal kitchen, outdoors – and shared by all.

The kitchen is on to supper. Among an ergonomic disaster of rickety tables, plastic bags, stacked boxes, pots and pans, a smooth-operating work triangle of veg-to-chopping-board-to-pan is in beautiful fuss-free motion. Wide-line noodles (sen yai) and deep pans of steaming stock foam over vast gas burners, and minutes later we dig in. Kaeng jeut, a simple comfort one-pot-noodle broth to which we add seasoned minced pork; deep-fried catfish with a hot-sour sweet dipping sauce; vegetable pancakes, stacked with a feathery leaf, served with a purply shrimp dip (with acquired flotsam whiff) and to go with everything, a big bowl of rice. Mr Boonpud then gets out his boat and off we khlong. Families are bathing in the waterways, soaping and scrubbing. Clambering in and out in their undies, from jetties and gaps in the thicket of ton-chak, clumps of massive palm frond that hedge the banks. Tall bamboos creak and bats skim the water as they graze on the dusk-dance of frenzied insects. The rush of the night air cools, then ahead flames cut the black. A deep rich molasses wafts, and we pass someone busy over a giant wok, where palmyra palm sugar, thick and dark, bubbles.

Idling on, the night bloom of something exotic, like the gentle perfume of a great aunt, blows in and trails the night air in diaphanous threads. Spirit houses twinkle from behind hefty straps of banana leaf. Above, the black tufts of coconut palm silhouette against a now prawn-pink sky, all slashed with chilli-red. Then magic happens, either side and aloft. On-off. On-off. On-off. It's as if the trees are bedecked with flashing Christmas lights. But it's fireflies, their little phosphorescent bottoms flashing, abdomens powered as if by some faulty generator. Then a massive sound system starts up, music blasts as loud as anything down Bangkok's Pat Pong. Thai mega-bass blasts through the black ghetto of palm. The fireflies respond, shaking their butts with radiant bleeps on every pulse, and a night full of bug life joins in, surround-sound, and volume whacked up. On this finale, we head back.

Before bed, I swim upstream. Up past where the tall giant bamboo stems creak.

Ban song Thai

It's dark. And the bats do dam-busters over my head. Coconuts and logs bob by. Water lettuce clumps bump and shiver. Land crabs side-scoot the mud banks and ghost away. The hours before – and now this. This, right here, right now. This is the moment of happiness. I could lose myself to the khlong.

3am. Cock-a-doodle-doo. Right in my ear. An unearthly hour wake-up call. I pray cock-a-doodle-don't. But it does. And then, as I feared, in the seconds it took me to fear, a ton of others join in. A caterwauling chorus amplified straight to my brain, from here, there, underneath and everywhere. And they carry on. Then the dogs join in at 6am. Then the whooping bird, the lesser greater spotted evil of them all. So I give up and get up. And nurse myself awake over a breakfast of preserved eggs and a soupy congee that I jolt into action with a seasoning of salt-dried mackerel. Delicious, but I was hungry for chicken, and the rest.

The waterways are the lifeblood of Samut Songkhram. Everyone and everything comes, goes, arrives and thrives by khlong. Monks make their morning paddle upstream and receive alms – food that is given out at the jetties. Here the corner shop is mobile; it comes to you. Palm-hatted women riding boats stacked with nibbly things sidle on up quietly, elegantly tinkling on little bells to announce their calling. One lady's boat is stuffed to the gunwales with flashy packets, fizzy drinks and household stuffs. As I look, with my camera, she whips out an instamatic and snaps a pic of me: 'Gotcha,' she nods, and beams triumphant.

I head off to Damnoen Saduak canal, and its Talaat Ton Khem floating market. It's a taxi-ride away in the next-door province of Ratchaburi, and I'm early to catch the buzz. Women work the water, gossiping with each other, in boats laden with piles and baskets of artfully arranged things. Money changes hands midstream and a melon and mangoes swap craft. Fruit (phon la mai) is what's mainly on offer: bananas, papaya, guava, kaffir limes, pomelo, jackfruit, rose apples, longan, mangosteen and maprang (an apricot-looking fruit with delicious sweet flesh). Other boats are kitted out as one-woman soup-and-noodle kitchens. Steam, chilli and nam pla builds into the morning air.

One women pulls up, sticks some Wendy-house-small seats on the wharf, then busies with her pans. A Pandora's box of bits and bobs are neatly arranged in bowls and baskets around her, ready for the off. It all looks too good. And I park-up too, pointing at what I want, while she chats to a chum pulled up alongside in another boat. With dexterity patterned by years of repeat, she leans, swivels and reaches, this way and that, and then pulls leafage and slippery rice noodles from a basket at the back of the boat, like a conjurer pulling a trick. There's some dunking of loaded wire baskets into steaming pots, then plop, as if presenting a rabbit out of a hat, a bundle of deliciousness lands in a bowl.

Next - and while still pulling faces with next door – she tops it with fried sliced tofu; crispy prawn, pre-fried in a shrimp dust-coat; crispy shallots; and crumbled toasted peanuts. Meanwhile, three more orders are taken, gossip continues, and I

don't exist. Yet the bowl of steaming goodness, now dressed with chopsticks and spoon, lands with a flourish right into my hand. My thank-you nod is not waited for – she's on to the next. I plaster on spoonfuls of chilli-ringed fish sauce and dig into a heavenly pond of noodle, Chinese kale (phak kha-naa) and fish balls. I move on for pud – lobes of mango piled on to a mulch of coconutty rice, khao niao mamuang. My lunch on the water now complete, I look up to find the morning melted away. The souvenir-laden boats are sweeping in, and before the inevitable hotel, motel, Holiday Inn tours arrive, I leave. To return to my home and dear chickens – in the coconut wood ◼

this is the moment of happiness

Glass noodle spring rolls with nam jim

Temple food I call it. Such delicate offerings should be eaten with the ritual of dips, leaves, herbs and wedges of tomato. Contrasts are all. Extra dipping sauces can make an appearance too, or a small saucer of fish sauce floated with rings of sliced hot chilli. An easy one. (See page 90).

```
5 tbsp caster sugar
100ml rice vinegar
1/2 tbsp finely chopped red chilli
salt
100g dried glass vermicelli noodles
20 spring-roll wrappers (not rice
  papers), about 15cm square
vegetable or groundnut oil
lettuce leaves, for wrapping (or cut
  pieces of banana leaf, for holding)
a small bunch Thai sweet basil
```

In a saucepan, stir together the sugar, rice vinegar and 3 tbsp water. Add the chilli, bring to a bubble then cook until reduced and syrupy. Lightly salt, leave to go cold, then pour into small dipping sauce bowls. Soak the noodles in a bowl of hot water for about 12 minutes, or until just soft, then drain, toss with a little salt and snip into 10cm lengths. To assemble the rolls, lay a spring-roll wrapper on a board, lay a bunch of noodles near the edge of one side, roll over once firmly to enclose the noodles, then fold in the two sides to overlap the exposed roll ends, and continue to roll up neatly and firmly. Moisten the remaining edge with a little water, gently firm together, then leave seam-side down on a tray. Do the same with all the wrappers - keeping the unrolled wrappers covered with a damp tea-towel to prevent them from drying out.

Heat a deepish pool of oil in a wok, then test it with a piece of spring-roll wrapper - it should gently turn golden brown and splutter when it hits the fat. Deep-fry the rolls in batches of five for about 3 minutes, then remove with a sieve, drain and rest on kitchen roll. Scoff wrapped in herb and leaf, dunking in sauces between each mouthful.

Wok-fried basil and chilli chicken

A Bangkok easy. You can't go wrong. Very tasty.

```
4 small skinned free-range chicken
  breasts, chopped
3cm piece fresh root ginger, peeled
4 hot red chillies, deseeded and
  roughly chopped
4 fat cloves garlic
4 coriander roots, scrubbed (optional)
salt
3 tbsp oil (vegetable or peanut)
2 tbsp finely chopped palm sugar
2 tbsp fish sauce
3 mild red chillies, deseeded and
  thickly shredded
big handful of Thai basil leaves
```

Briefly pulse the chicken breasts in a processer until coarse-minced but not mushed. Pound the ginger, chillies, garlic and coriander roots (if using) with a touch of salt to make a paste, then stir-fry in the oil in a wok for about a minute until it looks golden. Tip in the chicken and toss through and stir-fry until it browns, then stir in the sugar, and fry until things look sticky. Toss through the fish sauce and mild chillies, and stir-fry for a further minute or so, until the chicken is cooked. Shift from the heat, toss through the basil, and serve. Something to scoop up with is in order - crisp salad or trimmed tender cabbage leaves.

Khlong tom yam

This soup should taste hot and spicy-sour, and blowsy with fragrance. Prawns aren't the be-all here, so keep to veg if you don't eat creatures. Opens up the pores, so a perfect cool-off.

1.5 litres Asian chicken stock (see page 236)
2 sticks lemongrass, trimmed and smashed open
4cm piece fresh galangal or root ginger, peeled
  and thickly sliced
16 thin slices cooked bamboo shoots
8 kaffir lime leaves
3 tbsp fish sauce
juice of 2 limes
1 tbsp palm sugar or caster sugar
4 birdseye chillies, split
12 large cooked tiger prawns, shells on
4 small tomatoes, halved
handful of coriander leaf and stem, roughly chopped

Simmer the stock with the smashed lemongrass, galangal, bamboo shoot and half the lime leaves for about 8 minutes, then stir in half the fish sauce, half the lime juice, half the sugar and half the chillies, and leave to bubble for a couple of minutes. Next, shell the prawns, keeping the tail ends on, then add to the soup; if they're not cooked, simmer gently for 2 minutes or so. Discard the spent lemongrass and lime leaves, then stir in the tomato and remaining kaffir lime leaves, shredded. Give it a taste, then add more fish sauce, sugar and chilli until it's blended to your liking. Remove from the heat and stir in the remaining lime juice. Divide between the bowls and chuck on a little leafage. Extra ground chilli or, for those with a keener Thai tongue, toasted shrimp paste mashed with chilli, can be added at the table.

Comfort noodle soup

One to knock together with the remains of a roast – or use a couple of chicken pieces. Rice can be switched for noodles, and an egg yolk cracked into each bowl on serving. Makes breakfast. Your noodles and flaked chick will beg for a little dish of fish sauce floated with sliced rings of hot chilli – for that on-the-side oomph.

1 leftover cooked chicken carcass or
  some chicken pieces
salt
5cm piece fresh root ginger, peeled and
  thickly sliced
2 cloves garlic
5 fat spring onions, cut into short
  lengths
dried or fresh wide rice noodles
2 handfuls beansprouts (optional)
fish sauce and sliced chilli, to serve

If using a chicken carcass, pull the remaining meat from the bones and keep on one side. Break the carcass into bits and stick it in a saucepan, then fill the pan with around 2 litres water and give it a good salting (MSG too, if you like); if using chicken pieces, pop them into the same amount of water whole. Bring to a bubble, spoon off any gunk that floats to the top, then chuck in the ginger, garlic and half the spring onions. Turn down the heat, and leave to bubble very gently — more a sort of blipping murmur — for about 40 minutes, or until the chicken is cooked through. Strain the stock and discard all the bones and flavouring bits (keeping the meat, shredded, if you've used pieces). Add the remaining spring onions.

Dunk the noodles and beansprouts (if using) into a pan of boiling water until just softened — 1 minute or so for fresh noodles, around 3 minutes for dried — then scoop out with a sieve. Divide between your bowls, along with some shreds of cooked chicken, then ladle in the piping-hot spring onion stock.

Chatujak satay

Where there's a market there's satay. Sticks of something grilling, wafting and deliciously sticky. (See right).

500g skinned free-range chicken breast
  fillets, roughly chopped, or pork mince
1 tbsp finely chopped palm sugar or
  caster sugar
2 tbsp fish sauce
1 stick lemongrass, trimmed, outer
  leaves discarded, finely chopped
2 birdseye chillies, very finely
  chopped
6 kaffir lime leaves, finely shredded
  and chopped, or use finely grated
  zest from 2 limes
4 small shallots (preferably Thai),
  finely chopped
100ml coconut cream
1/2 stem fresh green peppercorns,
  chopped, or a good twist of black
  pepper
1 tbsp cornflour
vegetable or groundnut oil
bottled Thai sweet chilli dipping sauce
  and chopped coriander, to serve

If using chicken, put it in a processor and briefly pulse to make a coarse mince-like paste. Stir the sugar with the fish sauce until dissolved, then mix this with the lemongrass, chillies and lime leaves, and leave to infuse for about 15 minutes. Tip this mixture over the minced meat, along with the shallots, coconut cream and pepper and stir through, then sprinkle over the cornflour and thoroughly combine to make a paste. Chill the paste, covered, for an hour or so, or until firmed up, then mould the mixture around pre-soaked bamboo sticks, making slim sausage shapes, and refrigerate, covered, until ready to cook.

When ready to cook, brush the meat all over with oil and grill over hot coals or on a chargrill pan or under a hot grill, turning occasionally, until cooked through and golden. Get that dipping sauce out, and herbaceous things too, if you have them.

Coconut fish curry

This is your classic coconut curry. Cooked beef, chicken or duck could be swapped for fish. Your choice. Halved green beans could be swapped for aubergine too. (See page 104).

8 shallots (preferably Thai), 4 finely sliced,
  4 finely chopped
vegetable or groundnut oil
2-3 tbsp Thai red curry paste, bought or home-made
  (see page 236)
3 kaffir lime leaves, torn (optional)
1/2 tbsp palm sugar or caster sugar
2 tbsp fish sauce
2 x 400ml cans coconut milk
400ml light chicken stock (use fresh, instant or
  the Asian stock on page 236)
6 round baby Thai aubergines, halved (optional)
500g skinned fish fillet (white fish, reef fish
  or salmon)
12 cherry tomatoes
good handful of Thai basil leaves

In a wok, fry the sliced shallots in a shallow pool of oil until brown and crisp, then drain on kitchen roll. Strain out all but 2 tbsp of the oil. Fry the chopped shallots until softened, then add the curry paste and stir-fry until the paste darkens a little. Stir in the lime leaves (if using), the sugar and fish sauce, then tip in the coconut milk and stock, and bubble up. Gently allow to murmur for about 10 minutes, so all the flavours meld, adding the aubergine halfway through (if using). Cut the fish into small chunks and pop these in too, and gently cook for 2 minutes. Add the tomatoes and half the basil and cook for a further 3 minutes, or until the tomatoes begin to show signs of skin-burst. Taste, and add a dash of fish sauce if it needs salt. Ladle into bowls, scatter with the crisp shallots and remaining basil, and eat with rice.

COCONUT FISH CURRY, PAGE 102

Chang Pier noodle salad Yam wun sen

Pork and squid in a salad – who'd have thought it? It's glorious. Crumbled puffed rice cake adds the crunch factor here. However, the devils are tricky to find, so I suggest sprinkling with some bought crispy shallot instead – scrunched prawn cracker is good too. (See right).

200g bean thread/glass noodles
3cm piece fresh root ginger, peeled and chopped
4 cloves garlic
2 small shallots, chopped
2 birdseye chillies, deseeded and sliced
salt and pepper
vegetable oil
200g pork mince or sliced pork fillet
fish sauce
3 tsp caster sugar
200g cleaned and prepared squid, sliced
1/2 tsp chilli flakes
3 tbsp lime juice
2 heads dried white fungus, soaked in cold water
  until soft and drained (optional)
6 garlic chives, or 2 spring onions, chopped
handful of Thai basil leaves
crispy shallots or crumbled rice cracker
lettuce leaves and lime wedges, to serve

Soak the noodles in warm water until soft – about 30 minutes – then drain. Pound together the ginger, garlic, shallots and chillies with a touch of salt to make a coarse paste. Heat 1 tbsp oil in a wok, toss in the pounded paste and stir-fry a little, then tip in the pork, season with a tbsp of fish sauce, pepper, salt and the sugar and stir-fry until the pork is cooked. Scoop out. Add a dash more oil to the wok, then tumble in the squid and stir-fry until it turns opaque – about 1 minute. Add around 2 tbsp water towards the end of the frying time. Remove the wok from the heat and tip in the noodles, cooked pork and all the remaining ingredients except the lettuce leaves and lime wedges. Tumble together and taste, adding more fish sauce, sugar or lime if necessary. It should taste explosive. Serve with lettuce leaves and lime.

BROKEN FISH TRAP TOM YAM, PAGE 112

Chicken and mushroom soup `Tom kha kai`

Everyone's comfortable love, and big enough and easy enough to lunch with. (See right).

```
3cm piece fresh galangal or root
  ginger, peeled and finely sliced
2 x 400ml cans coconut milk
2 sticks lemongrass, trimmed
2 shallots, chopped
4-6 small hot red chillies
6 kaffir lime leaves
2 large chicken breasts, skinned
handful of oyster mushrooms
500ml Asian chicken stock (see page 236)
juice of 1/2 lime or lemon
1 tbsp fish sauce
caster sugar (optional)
handful of coriander leaves and
  shredded chilli
```

Plop the galangal or ginger into the pan with the coconut milk. Thwack each stick of lemongrass hard with a rolling pin to smash it open — but leave it intact — then lob these into the pan, too. Chuck in the shallots, then the whole chillies and half the lime leaves — lightly scrumpled, so that they release their flavour — and bring to a boil. Meanwhile, slice the chicken about 5mm thick, then chuck it in with the mushrooms and bubble away for about 3 minutes, or until cooked. Stir in the chicken stock and bring back to a bubble for about a minute, then turn off the heat and stir in the lime juice and fish sauce. Give it a taste. If it's too sharp, sweeten it with a tsp or two of sugar. Fish out and discard the spent lemongrass and lime leaves, then serve sprinkled with coriander, a few chilli shreds (if you fancy the perk) and the remaining lime leaves, finely shredded. Thais down it with rice.

Broken fish trap `tom yam`

Think rockpool/shrimper's net here – wayward bits of seafood. Chuck in stuff like clams, mussels, a prawn or crab claw, and nuggets of fish with the prawns, but cook for longer if necessary: gulf-inspired and fisherman's-pot-like, yet effortlessly elegant. Thais sometimes use smoked fish or mackerel to make a richer soup. One for dieters but equally fantastic for those who are not wasting time on such things. (See page 110).

```
1 small sea bream or other white fish,
  filleted, boned (keep the bones) and
  broken into pieces
2 sticks lemongrass, trimmed and
  smashed open
4cm piece fresh galangal or root
  ginger, peeled and thickly sliced
8 kaffir lime leaves
3 tbsp fish sauce
juice of 2 limes
1 tbsp palm sugar or caster sugar
4 birdseye chillies, split
300g raw shell-on prawns
handful of basil, coriander or chopped
  garlic chives
```

Simmer the fish bones in 1.5 litres of water, along with the smashed lemongrass, galangal and half the lime leaves for about 20 minutes, then sieve into a clean pan, discarding all the bits. Stir in half the fish sauce, half the lime juice, half the sugar and half the chillies, and leave to bubble for a couple of minutes. Add the prawns and the fish pieces and simmer gently for 2-3 minutes or so, until the fish is cooked. Give it a taste and add more flavourings until it's blended in heat and sourness to your liking. Remove and discard the lemongrass and spent lime leaves. Stir in the remaining fresh kaffir lime leaves, remove from the heat and add the remaining lime juice. Divide between bowls and top with leaves. Again, toasted shrimp paste mashed with chilli can be added at the table.

Stir-fried crab claws

The fattest, juiciest arms of dismembered spider crab are on the menu at Bangkok's Seafood Market restaurant (Soi Sukhumvit 24, Sukhumvit Road, Khlongtoey). Here, in neon-lit supermarket-like surroundings, you grab a trolley, stack it with gorgeous seafood pulled from a mile-long iced counter – an altar to some of Thailand's finest – then select some veg, and hand the lot over to a battery of wok-flaming cooks, who will cook it to your suggestion (but with their formulaic interpretation). The selection and freshness is stunning – and the prices are too. This dish has its claws dug gloop-deep in China – but that's Bangkok for you. Regular crab claws work beautifully too.

2 fat arms of spider crab or other
  crab claws
2 tbsp groundnut oil
5 cloves garlic, roughly chopped
4 red chillies, chopped
3cm piece fresh root ginger, peeled
  and shredded
1 stick lemongrass, trimmed and shredded
salt and pepper
1 tbsp black vinegar or rice vinegar
3 tbsp Chinese rice wine
1 tbsp caster sugar
1/2 tbsp cornflour, dissolved in
  2 tbsp cold water
bunch of spring onions, finely
  shredded, or chopped garlic chives

Cut the spider crab claws into 6cm sections and crack them by bashing them with a rolling pin. For regular crab claws, just bash with a rolling pin to crack them. In both cases, leave the shell on. Heat the oil, then chuck in the garlic, chillies, ginger and lemongrass and stir-fry until things take up a touch of colour. Throw in the crab, some salt and pepper and 2 tbsp water, and stir-fry further for about 2 minutes, then add everything else but the greenery and bubble up. Cook, stirring every now and then, for a further 2 minutes or so, or until the crab is cooked and things look good. Stir through half of the spring onion and serve with the rest thrown on top, and more pepper.

Green papaya and peanut salad `Som` `tam` `Thai`

Green papaya is unripe papaya, and has white firm flesh and green skin. If you can't find it, use unripe mango or a firm deseeded cucumber. Never use a regular ripe papaya.

5 cloves garlic
4 birdseye chillies, roughly chopped
2 large mild red chillies, deseeded and
  roughly chopped
pinch of salt
1 piled tbsp dried shrimp
1 large green papaya, around 300g,
  peeled, deseeded and shredded
1-2 tbsp fish sauce
juice of 2 limes
1 tbsp palm sugar or caster sugar

4 small tomatoes, halved, deseeded and cut
  lengthways into eighths
large handful of beansprouts
4 tbsp toasted crushed peanuts (see page 236)

Pound together the garlic and chillies with a pinch of salt in a pestle and mortar until crushed and pasty. Roughly pound in the dried shrimp and a small handful of the shredded green papaya, so that it's crushed but still chunky. Stir in the fish sauce, lime juice and sugar until dissolved. Tip into a bowl, then add the remaining papaya, the tomatoes, beansprouts and about 3 tbsp of the toasted peanuts and toss through until all is well coated. Serve sprinkled with the remaining crushed peanuts.

Floating market noodles
Kuai tiao luuk chin plaa

Small narrow boats, fitted out like mini soup kitchens, work the khlongs (waterways), dishing up soupy-noodle variations on a theme. Subtract ingredients you can't get and add those you have – it's one of those flexible jobs. Shredded cooked chicken, beef or pork, or boiled quails' eggs, can be substituted for fish balls or prawns. Remember, Thai soups are all about balance and play. So think: soft and crisp, sharp and sweet, hot and bland, and all making an appearance together. Prawns are to be eaten in the shell here.

400g firm, white skinned fish fillet (conger eel,
  monkfish fillet etc.)
salt
fish sauce
1 free-range egg white
12 small shell-on tiger prawns, heads discarded
1 tbsp vegetable oil
1 tbsp caster sugar
2 tsp ground dried shrimp (grind in a spice mill)
1.5 litres Asian chicken stock (see page 236)
200g rice noodles, any sort
2 handfuls beansprouts
2 pieces dried white fungus, soaked in water until
  soft, torn into chunks (optional)
2 handfuls chopped greens, such as Chinese
  broccoli, choi-sum or spinach
2 tbsp each of crispy fried shallots and toasted
  crushed peanuts (see page 236)
3 tbsp rice vinegar mixed with 3 sliced red
  chillies

Put the fish, plus a sprinkling of salt, 2 tsp fish sauce and the egg white into a processor and pulse-process to a paste. Mould the paste into walnut-sized ball shapes, put on a plate, cover and chill to firm up. Cook them in gently bubbling water for about 3 minutes, then drain. In a heavy all-metal pan, fry the prawns in the oil for about 1 minute. Then stir through 1 tbsp fish sauce and the sugar, and cook until caramelized and sticky. Dry them a little in a low warm oven until brittle, then toss them with the ground dried shrimp.

When ready to serve, bring the stock to a gentle bubble and another pan of water to the boil. Cook the noodles in the water pan, according to the packet's instructions, then scoop out with a sieve and distribute between four bowls. Put the beansprouts, fungus (if using) and greens in the sieve and dunk into the hot water for about 1 minute, then drain and divide between the bowls. Ladle over the hot stock and fish balls. Scatter with the sticky crisp prawns toasted crushed peanuts and crispy shallots, and alongside serve the chilli rice vinegar, some fish sauce and sweet chilli sauce or ground chilli, for all to pick, choose and add.

Bangkok chicken rice plate

White-cut chicken on rice, with its cool cucumber, rip-roar of coriander, bowl of broth and all-important dipping sauce, is my no.1 hawker's rice. It's one of those lessons in the deliciously bland, the punchy and the silken, with the cool and crunchy. And I bee-line for it as soon as I hit Bangkok. Forget the bars and temples, this is hedonist heaven. Any number of dipping sauces can be served with it. Just make it. (See right).

4 free-range chicken breasts, on the bone
salt
5cm piece fresh root ginger, peeled and thickly sliced
5 cloves garlic, halved
4 large spring onions, halved
600g jasmine or long-grain rice, washed
1 small cucumber, sliced
good bunch of coriander, thoroughly washed

Dipping sauce
3cm piece fresh root ginger, peeled and sliced
2 cloves garlic
2 tsp salt
2 tbsp rice vinegar
1 tbsp fish sauce
2 tsp caster sugar
2 tbsp groundnut oil
1 tbsp chilli shrimp oil (or use oil warmed with
  crushed dried chilli)

Submerge the chicken in a pan of well-salted water and bring to the boil, removing any collecting flotsam from the surface. Add the ginger, garlic and 3 of the spring onions, turn down to a gentle bubble, cover the pan, and cook for 15 minutes. Turn off the heat and leave to cool for 20 minutes, while the meat cooks through. Remove the chicken and strain the stock, discarding its spent flavouring bits. Remove the meat from the bone once cooled, and slice thickly crossways. Traditionally, the chicken is served at room temperature, so don't get anxious if it cools off (if you want it hot, reheat in the stock).

Cook the rice according to the Perfect steam-boiled rice recipe on page 236, but use some of the chicken stock instead of water. Meanwhile, for the dipping sauce, pound together the ginger, garlic and salt to make a coarse paste, and — if your bunch has them — include 4 scrubbed roots of the coriander. Then stir in the vinegar, fish sauce, sugar and the oils and divide between four dipping bowls.

Pour the remaining reheated broth into bowls, adding the remaining spring onion, chopped. Pile the rice on to plates with the chicken on top, add some cucumber and a nice wodge of coriander leaves, and serve each with broth and sauce on the side. Get out the chopsticks or forks (Thais use both) and start dunking, supping on the broth between mouthfuls of rice and chicken. The broth can be splashed on too.

Jungle tiger salad

I'm talking prawn here, not big cat. A refresher –
a Thai prawn cocktail. (See right).

**Tumble together everything but the
prawns, shallots and green shoots and
herbs, then leave refrigerated for a
good half hour or more, so that the
marriage of flavours starts to sing.
Then toss through everything else and
serve immediately.**

finely grated zest and juice of 2 limes
2 tbsp fish sauce
2 tsp finely chopped palm sugar or
  caster sugar
1 stick lemongrass, finely chopped
3cm piece fresh root ginger, peeled and
  shredded
1 mild red chilli, shredded
2 hot red chillies, very finely sliced
24 cooked shelled tiger prawns (tails
  can be left on)
6 small shallots (preferably Thai pink
  ones), sliced
small handful of garlic chives, chopped
1 tbsp finely shredded kaffir lime leaves
4 big handfuls Thai basil and coriander
  leaves (include chopped stems)

Hot, sweet, salty and sour wraps

Leaf wraps, mien kum, are sold by hawkers in their
components, neatly poly-bagged in kit form, for home
assembly. Wedges of fresh mango are also sold bagged with a
similar hot peanut sauce. Pre-shredded and toasted coconut
can be had from Thai food stores. It's table-assembly food. DIY
stuff. So platter up all the ingredients, then get piling, saucing
and folding.

20 cha phlu, betel or regular lettuce leaves
1/4 fresh coconut, flesh shaved into small shreds
  and pan-toasted
small handful of dried shrimp
handful of lightly toasted peanuts (see page 236)
4cm piece fresh galangal or root ginger, peeled
  and finely chopped
2 limes, finely chopped (skin on)
a few tiny hot chillies (optional)

Peanut jam sauce
3 cloves garlic
4 small shallots, chopped
5cm piece fresh root ginger, peeled, finely chopped
3 tbsp toasted crushed peanuts (see page 236)
3 tsp shrimp paste
2 tbsp fish sauce
4 tbsp finely chopped palm sugar or muscovado sugar

**For the sauce, blast the garlic, half
the shallots and half the ginger in a
processor until well chopped but not
mushed, then put with the next four
sauce ingredients and 200ml water in a
saucepan and bubble up until thickened,
sticky, dark and caramelized – about
10 minutes. Add a touch more liquid if
it sets too thick. Leave to cool.**

**Arrange all the remaining ingredients,
including the remaining shallots and
ginger, in separate little piles on a
platter, putting the peanut jam sauce
in a small bowl in the middle. To eat,
teaspoon a little of the sauce on to a
leaf, then pile on spare amounts of
everything else, fold around and eat.
Whole chillies are only for the
Scoville baptized and initiated.**

Laos

Laos
flavours

Laos is sandwiched between Vietnam and Thailand, capped by China and sealed by Cambodia in the south. Land-locked, Lao cooks have turned to their biggest asset, the Mekong. Fish, such as the mighty pa boeuk, are netted and hooked from the great river, where the mud banks are staged into sweeping steps and green-carpeted with runners of carefully tended greens. Every stitch of soil is cultivated, whether it be the mud of the Mekong or small, neat vegetable plots in backyards. There's the usual meat fare, including some unusuals, such as Indian buffalo, which is simmered in stews, while its skin is made into crispy snacks or air-dried and mixed with a chilli and galangal jam (jio bong). And there's a lot of exotic game, wild-caught creatures that the World Wildlife Fund for Nature perhaps would raise an eyebrow over. Laos' flavours are particularly close to those of its southern neighbours. The countries share a passion for the mix of the salty, hot, sour, bitter and sweet: fish sauce, chilli, lime juice, tamarind, lemongrass, mint, coriander and basil. Yet the way Lao cooks work them is different. Meats and fish are pounded, some blended to creams with roasted aubergine;

dressings are creamed with egg yolk or mixed with fried garlic pastes. Toasty flavours and mushed concoctions are their thing – not always to Western tastes. Yet there's also grilled chicken (ping kai) and fish (ping paa) and roast duck (ping pet). Khao niau, or sticky rice, is the staple of every meal, and is eaten with everything, including salad. Morning rice noodle soup, foe, is served like the Vietnamese pho, with a platter of lettuce, coriander, mint, basil and mung beans and some green bean-like veg. Yet in Luang Prabang this comes with a toasted sesame paste too. Khao piak sen is another noodle soup, made with plump round rice noodles jumbled with pork or chicken and annointed with a dab of crushed ginger. And there's khao pun: noodles with a spiced coconut sauce and grilled slivers of meat. Homes are fairly sophisticated in towns, yet most still cook outdoors, and over charcoal. Houses may have mod-cons, but kitchen stoves are still just sticks and fire, and open to the elements. Specialities are: river moss (khai paen) sheets of dried algae (like nori), gathered from the Mekong, pressed with slivers of sun-dried tomato and polka-dotted with toasted sesame seeds, briefly deep-fried and served crisp with drinks; aw lam, a spicy soup with a bitter-sour flavour, floated with oyster mushrooms and herbs; a watercress salad tossed with a toasted flavour egg dressing, and generous spicy green papaya salads accompanied by airy pork scratchings. Bush-tucker trials are up for grabs too. Curiosities, let's say. You're either a bug-loving traveller, or you're not. There are no half measures when it comes to Indochine unusuals. The local market has innocent-looking sections of bamboo on offer, yet inside vast fat grubs cocoon, ready to be charcoal-roasted, tucked up as they are. Then there's a taste for the untamed — squirrels, civets, monitor lizards, bats and rats — which all make an appearance at the Talaat Naviengkham market. Up-river, at the Pak Ou caves, little girls offer deep-fried fledglings rowed up on sticks to the disembarking tourists — who on identification act like they've trodden in something, and then scatter. Remember to tread carefully with paa-daek (or 'padek') though, the extra pungent fish sauce that is made from fermented chunks of fish and rice dust, for further south it can contain liver flukes from infected fish.

kitchen stoves are still just
sticks and fire

talking drums and bells, riding

on the sweat of a jungle night

and the snake of the Mekong — the river of
    novels, red-brown and wide — comes into view

The Vientiane Domestic flight had been a long wait – an endless munch through packets of things, sat in uncomfortable warmth with mosquito spray in hand. Now up we bob, in a 12-seater, propelling northward above cloud and jungle, across mountainous Laos, heading for its ancient capital, Luang Prabang, in a knackered set of wings that buzzes cumbersomely like a mossie that's drunk more than its fill. An airy little craft that has me praying to God for the first time since school. After an hour of splutter and whirr, we dive-bomb and my heart big-dippers. Green flashes up, hills of it. Yet we sail unscathed through a pass layered with jungle on jungle, and the snake of the Mekong – the river of novels, red-brown and wide – comes into view. Descending fast, wobbling like a duck with its undercarriage ready to tread water, we seek tarmac. The great river ribbons through the jungling folds beyond. Not a runway in sight.

Then thump, and a clang. And I wake, remembering. Remembering where I am. We'd landed (safely, I must add), I'd unpacked, eaten and settled, then drifted off. It's now 4am and I'm wide awake in the early hours, lying in bolstered comfort in the Apsara Hotel, transported to new time and new place. Thump, thump and clang comes again. The sounds of heavy hide and iron, talking drums and bells, riding on the sweat of a jungle night. Luang Prabang's monks are drumming in the new half-moon at dawn.

Road travel to and from Vientiane was once 'not advised'. Bandits. But now the territories are pretty much okay, and it's open game for the traveller. Flying here still saves the sore-bottom deal of a long and bumpy ride though. And I'd certainly arrived. 'On the Yak plane?' asks ex-Saatchi & Saatchi Maggie Elsdon, clutching the top of her palm hat, looking skyward, with other arm flaying drunken, pointing in some vague direction of Luang Prabang's smidgen of airstrip. 'Or was it the ATR?' she quickly follows, dancing around on the spot, as her transvestite next-door neighbour pegs out the washing (only an ex-ad London girl could pitch up in the back-end-of-beyond next door to a boy in make-up and wedges). She's here to fix up the Apsara's interior look. Her ad world now traded in for Yaks, trannies, temple cushions, silks and paint.

The historical centre to Luang Prabang – or Muang Luang, as the locals call it – straddles an isthmus of land, sandwiched between two rivers, the Mekong and the Nam Khan. Isolated by its geography and warring conflicts, it has, until of late, been cut off from the world. Under wraps, and thus unspoilt. UNESCO has now labelled it a world heritage site, and so the locals battle for the right to live a 21st-century existence of satellite dish, concrete and mast. The place lounges, like some dosing and exotic Pre-Raphaelite nymph, laid back in her watery bed. The only unrestful displays are from its cockerels, which grumble as they peck each other around town. Old houses on stilts and 1920s colonial Lao-French stucco and wood homes sit side-by-side with more modern corrugated creations, amid palms, hardwoods, datura plants and zany-bright flowering shrubs. On the outskirts of town, salad gardens are laid out with Beatrix Potter charm: in patchworks of leafy checks.

Lettuces and stuff Peter Rabbit would kill for are laid down in quilts of lushness, complete with stream, and narrow mud paths for small feet.

Each morning at dawn, the pound of pestle on mortar can be heard from behind shuttered doors. Kettles steam on fires. And on cue, the novice monks rise, bang their drums, and pass barefoot through the streets collecting their alms – their free meals – to take back to their temple quarters. Wat Xieng Thong is the town's prettiest temple, and with its low slopey roofs it has to be the Hansel and Gretel of temples. At 500 years old, it takes the biscuit, for those who like their gingerbread in gold frieze and mirror mosaic.

What with Luang Prabang's monks-in-the-making and its 32 temples, it's very much a holy centre, and all can be poked around in relative quiet. But here the picture book closes. Indulge, but remember the civil and international bloody conflicts that were, until quite recently, Laos' plague. A wander around the Royal Palace offers a reminder of those so recently lost. Barefoot, you walk through rich rooms, treading the deep polish of time, with the imperial creak underfoot. You move between heavy silk divans, cabinets of chess-set sized buddhas and rare bits and bobs, on through reception rooms hung with big portraits. King Savang Vatthana and his family hang here, dressed in 1970s brocades, while their starved bones lie lost in some Communist re-education camp up north. Unwanted lives, chattels and memory now lie cordoned and behind rope. Beautiful heritage robbed of beautiful end ∎

Luang Prabang

Behind a bamboo fence in a glory of sparkly lights is a restaurant without a sign. It serves one thing, sin daad (meat barbecue). Holes have been hewn out of melamine-topped tables, as if in a crazed moment the owner thought 'must-have-meat-barbecue-restaurant, and now'. In each busted hole, a brazier of hot coals is placed, then a metal perforated dish – a car hub-cap thing – is sat on top. Alongside this is placed a small steel bucket of steaming stock, a basket bundled with plant stuff – swamp spinach (morning glory), oyster and wood-ear mushrooms – and eggs. Plus a dish of lime wedges, chopped garlic, a hot chilli paste and a platter of carpaccio-thin buffalo meat and some pork fat. So much raw ingredient, it's as if a slice of the morning market has arrived. A nugget of fat is placed in the middle of the metal grill to slow-render and baste the cooking plate. Fat deltas and trickles, further flavouring the broth that's ladled in at the edge – where veg and cracked eggs are popped in to poach. We stick on the buffalo and splash on fish sauce and the meat's fringes hiss. Through wafts of intense steam and smoke, pump the sounds of Blue's 'All Rise' on a loop. We scoop soup and soft-yolk eggs into our bowls, stick on the grilled meat, with squeezes of this and sploshes of that. Our hub-cap hob makes a groovy night out ◾

Restaurant no name

Out of town, sat at a table on a concrete concourse, amid ill-fed and life-weary pot plants, comes some glorious Lao food at the Malee restaurant, from a menu titled 'Luang Prabang Novrishment'. It's divided into – unintentionally entertaining – sections, such as 'Cutting up into small pieces'. With dishes such as 'Boiled the fish with the big onion'; 'Stuffing fist and cappage'; 'Grinded crap pepper sauce'; 'Soft-boiled pig entrails salad', and to drink – 'Picked drug alcohols 11 Tiger brand'. Reads like some 'wanted column' cannibal's private dining dungeon credentials. Smells fantastic. The drug leafy thing sounds good – and we down eggcupfuls of a musty whisky-like brew. On the food front, I go for greens with a caramel dipping sauce, pungent with paa-daek. An elderly Thai hen-party arrives, scoffs, and is gone – and before we've caught a whiff of our firsts. Then comes 'chicken laap' (minced chicken and banana flower salad), and then banana leaf steamed fish on the bone, a muddy-sweet dab hooked fresh from the Mekong and now stacked with dill. On opening it's a pulp of bones and flesh and so, like a mouthful of stickleback, a minefield to eat but gorgeous still, with its perfume of dill, kaffir lime and ginger. Cutting up into small pieces: here makes for less fast-food and more slow-food eating. 'Pass the crap pepper sauce. And more picked drugs please, before I face the stuffing fist. Cheers' ◾

Malee Laos food

SPICY GREEN PAPAYA SALAD WITH
BASIL AND MINT, PAGE 145

Cashews, lime and spring onion

The stuff of pre-dinner snifters and sundowners on the terrace. The Apsara Hotel, Luang Prabang, dishes these up as you sit, G&T in hand, next to the cool of the Nam Khan river.

```
vegetable oil
200g unroasted unsalted cashew nuts
sea salt
3cm piece fresh root ginger, peeled and finely shredded
4 spring onions, shredded, or small bunch of garlic chives
juice of 1 lime
```

Heat a shallow pool of oil in a wok, then slip in the nuts and gently fry until they've turned to gold. Strain off the oil, then sprinkle the nuts well with sea salt and the shredded ginger, and stir-fry for about 30 seconds. Remove from the heat, stir through the spring onions, then pour over the lime juice. Toss through and spill on to a plate or into a bowl. A grating of lime zest will pump-up-the-volume further (I do). Eat while still fragrant and warm.

Lemongrass fish salad with chilli and lime
Goi pa laap

Using finely chopped, grilled chicken breast with shredded banana flower, instead of fish, is a Luang Prabang variation. As is minced beef (buffalo), like tartare, with the addition of fennel seeds and galangal, which in true Laos spirit would come under the hammer of the pestle and be pulverized to something sticky-pasty. The locals would eat this with slices of cucumber and sticky rice – and sometimes lettuce leaves, for wrapping up mouthfuls. Crispy shallots or spring onions can be bought in packets from Oriental stores, and will cut corners. (See left).

```
500g trout or carp or other white fish
  (such as sea bass, snapper) fillets
salt and white pepper
3 sticks lemongrass, trimmed and
  finely shredded
4 kaffir lime leaves, finely shredded
vegetable oil
6 fat cloves garlic, finely sliced
4 shallots, sliced and left to dry a
  little
5 tbsp lime juice
2 tbsp fish sauce
2 tsp caster sugar
1 tbsp toasted ground rice (see page 236)
1/2 tsp cayenne pepper
2 mild red chillies, deseeded and
  finely shredded
bunch each of Thai basil and coriander
```

Wash and rinse the fish, then salt and pepper all over, put on a plate and either steam for 8 minutes or cover with clingfilm and microwave until cooked through – then leave to cool. Flake the meat from the bones and discard the skin. Next, fry the lemongrass and lime leaves in a little oil until slightly frazzled and softened, then drain on kitchen roll. Then fry the garlic until golden – but don't let it darken – and drain in the same way. Then fry the sliced shallot until crisp, and drain.

Mix the flaked fish with everything above and all the remaining ingredients. Taste and add more fish sauce if it needs a further salting. Divide into four portions and serve with a little more ground rice and shredded chilli scattered on top.

Temple aubergine with sweet chilli shrimp sauce

You can either fry, roast or grill the aubergine. If roasted or grilled, the skin should be stripped off afterward and tossed away, and a Lao cook would pound the flesh to a paste (like babaganoush). Anything melting in the aubergine department is temple food for me, and – just-like-a-prayer – this'll take you there. Monks love it too. (See right).

2 tsp shrimp paste
3 cloves garlic
2 tbsp chopped shallots
5 red birdseye chillies, chopped
5 dried mild red chillies
groundnut oil
2 tbsp finely chopped palm sugar or
  caster sugar
1 1/2 tbsp fish sauce
3 tbsp lime juice
3 narrow violet or 2 regular aubergines
2 tbsp dried shrimp, ground to powder
handful of chopped spring onion, fresh
  mint or fresh coriander

Wrap the shrimp paste in a small square of foil, squashing it flat, then toast in a dry hot pan for a few minutes. Pound the toasted shrimp paste with the garlic, shallots and chillies until pasty, then fry in 2 tbsp oil until it darkens a little. Stir in the sugar and bubble up until it starts to look even darker, then stir in the fish sauce and lime juice, bubble up again, remove from the heat, and leave to go cold.

Cut the aubergines into long round sections — if using regular aubergines cut them into quarters lengthways and then into shorter lengths — and deep-fry in a wok in a generous pool of oil until just cooked through (or roast, see introduction). To retain their purple-skinned colour, make sure the aubergines are kept dunked while frying. Drain, then serve spooned with the sauce (or put it into dipping bowls), and rain with the ground shrimp and the herby bits.

Spicy green papaya salad with basil and mint
Tam maak-houng

The lightest of pork scratchings, as airy as prawn crackers, should accompany this one, the perfect antidote to the sharpness and crunch of the salad. But not essential. A powerful and pungent fish sauce, paa-daek, is used by Laotians in their dressing. I suggest adding a touch of crushed dried shrimp to regular fish sauce if you really want to score goals. They'd throw in some maak kawk, a sour olive-shaped fruit, too (no, you're not expected to find that one). (See page 139).

4 red birdseye chillies, deseeded and
  roughly chopped
3 fat cloves garlic
1/2 tsp salt
2 tsp caster sugar
1/2 tbsp dried shrimp
350g green papaya, peeled, deseeded and
  finely shredded

handful of baby purple Thai aubergines,
  halved (optional)
lime juice, to taste
2-3 tbsp fish sauce
8 small tomatoes (baby plum are good),
  skinned and halved
handful each of Thai basil and mint
puffed pork scratchings (optional;
  available from Chinese food stores)

Pound together the chillies and garlic with the salt until crushed and pasty. Pound in the sugar and dried shrimp, then add a small handful of the papaya and crush until pasty. Add the aubergines and very lightly bash, so they're lightly crushed but still chunky, then stir through the lime juice, fish sauce and tomatoes. Tip the mixture into a bowl, then add the remaining shredded papaya and the herbs and toss through until all is well coated and mixed. Pork scratchings on the side, and you're away.

Laos sticky rice
Khao niaw

Sticky rice, brought to table in a round hat-box-shaped basket, is the foundation of all – and eaten with all. The rice is scooped and, with the same hand, formed into small balls, then rolled into the food. Like a magnet, it picks up all morsels and sauces in its path. Lao cooks steam their rice in a cone-shaped basket sat over a pot – you can use a regular steamer, lined with muslin or cheesecloth. Black sticky rice is popular too. (See right).

2 cups glutinous rice, soaked for
  6 hours or overnight in cold water

Drain the rice and rinse it under cold water, then spread it out over a muslin-lined steaming tray. Assemble your steamer with plenty of water in the base pan, then cover and steam for about 25 minutes, or until the rice is cooked. It should still have some bite, yet be sticky. Scoop out (and no rinsing, God forbid) and serve in a basket or bowl, or on a plate.

Luang Prabang garden salad

Watercress, something we think of as being so cool-climate British, grows effortlessly and in quantity in Luang Prabang's vegetable plots. It's one of their best-loved leaves, just like it is ours. It's their dressing that makes this wondrous – the mix of toasted garlic oil and creamed egg yolk. A splosh of the old soy sauce is good in it too. Swap the cucumber for sliced Asian pear, if you know where to get it: very Laos. (See right).

4 free-range eggs, hard-boiled and separated into yolks
  and whites
1 small ridged cucumber, finely sliced
8 small plum tomatoes, halved
2 bunches watercress, any coarse stems removed
small bunch each of mint and coriander, leaves only
small bunch of spring onions, chopped

Dressing
2 cloves garlic, finely chopped
4 tbsp vegetable or groundnut oil
2 cooked egg yolks (from the eggs above), crushed to a paste
3 tbsp lime juice
1 tsp caster sugar
salt and white pepper

To make the dressing, fry the garlic in the oil until it turns a nut brown (but don't scorch it, otherwise it will turn bitter), then leave the oil to go cold. Next, add the remaining dressing ingredients to the garlic oil and pound or beat together until the liquids have homogenized with the egg yolks. Taste for seasoning, and add more salt if needed.

To assemble the salad, slice the egg whites into halves or quarters, then pile with the remaining ingredients into shallow bowls or on to plates, then spoon over the garlic and egg dressing.

Toasted caramel dipping sauce

Dipping and dunking material for wilted veg, fried slices of aubergine and/or sticky rice. The Malee restaurant, on the outskirts of Luang Prabang, serves it with a platter of floppy greens and stems of wilted sprouting broccoli – almost like home.

```
4 fat cloves garlic, chopped
4 mild red chillies, deseeded and chopped
1 tsp salt
2 tbsp fish sauce
2 tbsp caster sugar
1 tbsp fried garlic oil (fry 2 chopped garlic cloves in
  2 tbsp vegetable oil until nut-brown)
2-3 tbsp lime juice
2 tsp toasted sesame seeds
```

Pound the garlic and the chillies with the salt to make a paste, then add 1 tbsp water and the fish sauce and mix together. Put the caster sugar into a small saucepan, then melt on a gentle heat until it caramelizes. Allow to cool a little, then stir in the paste and the garlic oil, and boil up again. Stir in the lime juice and leave to cool, then sprinkle with toasted sesame seeds.

Hot and sour oyster mushroom and pumpkin soup Gaeng juet

Clumps of oyster mushrooms, their bone-white gills as delicate as porcelain, are lovingly arranged and displayed in baskets by the ladies of Luang Prabang's Talaat Naviengkham morning market. Their silken slipperiness is the stuff of broth dreams. Whack in some herbage on serving. (See right).

1 litre Asian chicken stock (see page 236)
2 sticks lemongrass, trimmed and smashed
3cm piece fresh galangal, sliced
3 kaffir lime leaves, ripped
3 shallots, halved
4 tbsp tamarind water (see page 236)
salt
200g peeled firm pumpkin, cut into small chunks
12 small oyster mushrooms, stems trimmed
4 small tomatoes, halved
small handful of garlic chives or
  2 spring onions, sliced
bowl of mixed herbs and lime halves, to serve

Put the stock, lemongrass, galangal, lime leaves, shallots, tamarind water and a dash of salt into a saucepan and bring to a bubble, then simmer, covered, for about 10 minutes. Fish or strain out all the flavouring ingredients, discard them, then taste, adding more salt if the stock needs it. Add the chopped pumpkin to the stock and allow to gently bubble until the pumpkin is almost tender. Next, throw in the mushrooms and gently poach for about a minute, then add the tomatoes and the garlic chives. Bubble up, then ladle into four bowls. More herbs can be added at the table — doled out in help-yourself little bowls.

Vietnam

Vietnam
flavours

Neighbours and invaders have all had a hand in Vietnamese food: the Chinese in the north; Thailand, Cambodia and Laos in the west; and then the world that trooped in by sea, via its vast strip of coast. Pho bo (beef soup noodle) is a good example of assimilation, as its stock spices — star anise, cinnamon, ginger, and clove — arrived from Indonesia and the Middle East, and the eating of beef was unheard of until the 20th-century, as cows and buffalo were for field work, not slaughter. The French occupation left stylish legacies: the baguette, pâté, crème caramel, and coffee — and some lingo for bicycle parts and kitchenalia. The Americans left bullet holes, sorrow, and ice-cream. Lapped by the sea and saturated by its two vast deltas, the Mekong and the Red River, Vietnam's geography has put on its plate a rice and seafood diet to kill for. Spicing has not the wham-bam smack of Thai belief, but is gentle, popping up in marinades (especially if things are to be preserved), and the Vietnamese only add heat in dribs and drabs as they eat. Stewing or slow-braising is the common practice, as it deals with the thrift factor admirably: things slow-cooked in liquid swell and flavour others, whereas things grilled or roasted diminish and give nothing. It's stove-top cooking, in a wok, pot or over charcoal. Ovens don't exist. Nuoc mam (fish sauce and its offspring of fermented seafood sauces), made from fermented fish and salt, is the all-important salt seasoning and dipping sauce. Then come lime juice, lemongrass, garlic, chives, ginger, galangal, sugar and chilli, and in smaller amounts, turmeric, star anise, cinnamon and five-spice. Toasted crushed peanuts, dried shrimp and herbs such as mint, roushong (like mint), betel leaves and coriander, put on food on serving, are vital for punch and texture. There's a logic to all the tailorings and matchings. For instance, rice paddy herb is chucked into fish soups to make them less fishy; boiled duck is eaten with gingered fish sauce for digestive reasons; shellfish are regarded as a cold food and must be eaten with hot spices such as pepper, and meat is used frugally as it's pricy, so dishes have evolved without the need for it. Ketchups beyond fish sauce are de rigueur too: northerners love pickled aubergine and fermented soy bean; those further south plump for thinner salt-fermented sauces made from seafood.

Breakfast is a carb fest. In Hanoi, pho (starchy rice noodles) with slivers of meat in broth provide the energy for a day's work, and are eaten on the street; in Hoi An, the morning street stalls serve steamed sticky rice and mung beans topped with sugar and peanuts, tipped into a banana leaf cone. Tea time is street time too, with dishes such as the banh bot loc - dumplings of cassava flour stuffed with pork and shrimp, customarily dressed and sprinkled - dished up outside Hoi An market. The bland and the soft with the crunchy. Seafood is big time everywhere and at any time of day. What with all that coast, delta and paddy acreage, it's no wonder. And now for something different. Vietnamese do this best. Their exotic titbits are not for mimsies: roast dog; fruit bat which hangs upside down, flexing big arm-pits, claws and teeth; cobra with all its various live beating bits; or indeed a snifter of human placenta wine. Be bold. Eat from the street. It's the only way to taste Vietnam, and you are less likely to get stomach troubles, for you can see the set-up. Foods freshly boiled or fried before you score top marks. So pull up a stool and enjoy the banter, the comings-and-goings and the delicious things.

For the next course, move in further amidst the clatter and scrape of tin bowl, and the squawk, thud, crack and slice of fowl and veg on block.

Fat drips. Smoke drifts. Steam curls, plumes and snakes, then wafts and dissipates into the eaves of Sapa's Saturday covered market. Well-sharpened blades cut through green stems. Chopping boards thud. Baskets of noodles are dunked and tipped into bowls of beansprouts and shredded meat. Hands reach for chopsticks, and herbs are scooped and mulched in. Spoons sauce; bowls are at faces, and benches are full. Through the mist of smoking charcoal-grilled bun cha (bamboo skewered pork) and the steam of pho (noodle broth), people, dressed as if straight out of the pages of National Geographic – in silver-hooped neckwear, wrapped headgear and striking colour – are totally focused. On food. It's a scene unchanged for centuries, yet now appears like a futuristic film set, a mix of past and present, in fantastical and displaced costumery even Ridley Scott couldn't dream up. The tribespeople of the Lao Cai Province in north-eastern Vietnam, the Black H'mong in metallic inky-blue hemp with leg warmers and large jewellery, and the Dzao women, with shaven foreheads, in their coins, tassels, red turban garb and flashing gold teeth, all tuck into breakfast.

It took 11 dusty hours of trucks, blips and jars on dodgy bits of camber, to ascend to this niche in the world. A corner 350 kilometres north of Hanoi, and next to the China borders, where you and I are still, just about, a novelty. Lost worlds take a trek to reach: through foothills, passes and mountains, negotiating precipitous earthworks, with bulldozers now carving a broader route; through spectacular vistas with backdrops brushed lush with chameorops fan palms, banana, hardwoods and bamboo forest, with stems as thick as your leg; through thickly forested slopes – phototropic battlegrounds of green on green; and skirting rocky outcrops frayed with gangly pine, spliced here and there with liquid terracotta – the snake of the Red River – leading us on and on, and up and up.

In the foothills we pass little thatched Tai tribe homes on stilts, rice paddies in contoured tiers, woven boats on ponds, troops of school kids, cycles and carts with precision-wrapped loads and water buffalo prodded by women elegant in coolie hats. Moving higher, the bamboo forests give way to alpine and dark green sprucy things. Temperatures cool, ecosystems change, palms and coolie hats are gone. Mists fug the mountain peaks and the slopes undulate like folds of coniferous-green chenille. The air bears the soul of the hardy, the woody, of smoke and earth. And as the curtain of evening blows in, suppers simmer, and the kippered thatch on homes seeps smoke.

The town of Sapa sprang up in the 1920s as a hill station. It now resembles a curious blend of Disney-meets-French colonial. Buildings are honey-orange, their concrete balustrades painted in an assortment of 1970s bathroom-suite-pampas. Tourist joints boast pizza. My hotel, The Bamboo, has a piped muzak dining room, child waiters, and a disco bar called Apocalypse Now. The fish hotpot here is the only original and delicious thing: dark and warm, rich with anise, cinnamon, soy-stewed belly pork and chunks of sugar cane, with a slab of river fish rafting on top. And my window has a five-star view: it looks out on Fransipan Mountain, the highest in Vietnam, its surrounding hills and dales home to the tribes.

Migrating from China into Vietnam over the last three centuries, the montagnards (hill tribes), have made the most of its inhospitable areas, fleeing Kuichou in China, after various waves of failed resistance to Chinese government, to make their home in an equally unwelcoming Vietnam. They still lead semi-nomadic lives and, despite more recent government declarations to the contrary, are still quietly persecuted by the police for their monotheistic beliefs. The H'mong people, in all their varieties, are particularly out-and-about and noticeable: the Do (who wear white), Du (black), Sua (blue), Si (red) and the Senh (the flower H'mong, whose women sport plaid wool headdresses). But you'll need some form of Identikit to tell one from another, for determining correct nomenclature can be merely down to how they might wear their buttons. Travelling into Sapa at the weekends, the H'mong come with tall woven baskets worn back-pack style, with sugar cane and clothes to sell, to depart with umbrellas and Walkmans plugged to ears.

That evening, I head to the street by the church, where night hawkers grill corn cobs, cassava and sweet potatoes over coals, and I eat something hot. But the outdoorsiness, humbleness and darkness of it all make it everything. My guidebook hints this to be Sapa's night time 'Love Market', where tribespeople canoodle under the stars. No longer.

A river runs through it

The 'Love Market' now is given over to techno and strobe at Apocalypse Now.

East of Sapa lies Bac Ha. A weird spot. Dogs bark and lope about. Streets are wide and empty, flattened by December chill, and houses silent. The few who are out are in thick clothes. I unpack for jumpers – in a hotel room, that's ruched with synthetic lacy drapes that would rival a piccaninny's Sunday best. The Khach San Sao Mai hotel is Vietnamese-tries-its-hand-at-chalet style and multi-storey – pine-clad and out-of-sorts sinister. It's all sharp corners and edges. Spooky. Suddenly, and more spookily, 'Hello' comes a familiar voice, across the rooftops, and in through the open window '...is it me you're looking for?' It's dear old Lionel Ritchie, on the town's loudspeaker system. This, and other unwanted stuff, babbles on and off all day, and pipes up in the very early hours.

Bac Ha's aesthetic is its Sunday market. Droves of pony-riding tribespeople come to sell and trade buffalos and pigs, amid a lot of push and shove. As at Sapa, a carnival of race and ethnic mix gathers here, like a world of costume dolls sprung to life. Buffalo boys are fired up with the local brew, an intoxicating liquor made from fermented corn, and the girls are on to tea. Mums feed starchy rice noodles to plump and papoosed babies by the chopstickful. Like cuckoo chicks, they suck in their white worms, eyes closed. Vast pots are on the boil again in the covered areas, and hot rice pancakes with palm sugar, wrapped take-away in banana leaves, can be had in the open alleys. Leaf soups steeped with celery are doled out,

and mounded with minced pork or chicken; tofu tumbled in stock is doused with mint, chilli flakes and rings of orange chilli fished from nuoc mam (fish sauce). I eat pho ga, chicken noodle soup, at a long, low, wood table. A scant bit of bird cleaved with bones and all, delicious, but amateur stuff in comparison to those draining soups steeped with pig and buffalo blood, parked up by the platter of anatomically correct entrails on my right.

Next day, I'm back on the Red route. Following that river again, by car, all the way back to Hanoi, then out of town and to the Gulf of Tonkin – three and a half hours and 160 kilometres east, where the river deltas into Vietnam's number one beauty spot, Halong Bay. So close to China's borders that the place now crawls with the Chinese world and his wife, Vietnam's latest wave of day-trippers. They feast on the crustacea at the waterfront restaurants, splitting crabs and sucking on sea things of scant meat. Unlike the rest of Vietnam, soups here are thickened with cornflour, there's the whiff of oyster sauce in the air, and the fish sauce is not out. At breakfast they're hell-bent on bowls of congee. An old woman, with plucked eyebrows that resemble snakes, plugs in a whole 1,000-year-old egg, pushing her jaw forward to take it like a cobra with a rodent. The rest, like wildebeest at a watering-hole, noisily slurp.

I make for a boat. The patter of tiny Chinese feet is not far behind, and they soon set sail in an armada of camera flashes. We arrive at some grottos where a tiny man attached to a huge megaphone blasts all atmosphere to

oblivion. Stalactites resembling lions and dragons (a favourite naturally, but pushing it) are pointed out, yet it looks more Gaudi Sagrada Familia Gothic. Folds of rock, like chamois leather, hang from the roof and it's all very lovely, if you like that sort of thing. This is the first, last and only stop for the Chinese. Once they've been marched through and seen a rock or two, they return to the mainland. My pleasure-boat ducks all gone, peace and seclusion returns to the bay's 3,000 islands, in mists that refuse to pull back. The towering rocks dissolve into greys, like cut-outs being wheeled in and out of a Kabuki theatre set. A silent one-manned fishing boat occasionally enters the scene stage left or right, and that's it. Halong Bay settles back into the silence of ages ∎

air bears the
                soul of
smoke and earth

i buy a blue disposable bag mac

Up a steep flight of well-trodden stairs, I reach a dusky neon-lit room. The owner sits me down at a pale-green, melamine-topped table next to a large open window. The view is of angry electricity cable and Christmas lights and hammer and sickle motifs string the street. Below, thousands of tidily turned-out kids in ties and crisp shirts mill towards a concert, waving red national flags, their gold stars festive with light. Above me, a gravity-defying shrine juts, table-like, out of the wall on high, displaying little cabinets of gods, incense, and fake roses in a blue-and-white china vase, all coated in a delicate bloom of cooking fat. Nothing cools, as it's as hot in as it is out. All is as clogged as the glaze on the vase. There's no menu, no choice, and no luxuries. Yet I've made it, just before closing, in time for the most heavenly herby noodled thing on earth. At Cha Ca La Vong, a restaurant in Cha Ca Street, Hanoi, they dish up only one thing: cha ca (grilled fish with noodles).

The fug of the heat muffles the buzz of moped, wall-mounted fans hopelessly whirr, and minutes later, a tray of gloriousness arrives: springy piles of rice vermicelli (bun) on little blue plates; toasted crushed peanuts; a plate of soft herbs, damply warm and fragrant; a little bowl of fish sauce bobbing with rings of orange chilli and a charcoal-filled burner with a pan of spluttering cha ca atop, acid-vibrant with turmeric. Next, a bowl brimming with bustingly-green dill, enough to turn me happily ruminant, is tipped over like a thatch, then mulched through. It wilts and wafts dill gorgeously all over the shop. Dizzy to get at it, I thrust some noodles into my bowl, spoon on the dilled fish, then plonk herbs, peanut and some flotsamy splashes of deliciously whiffy sauce, leaving dribbles, leaf and stray noodle in my wake. And in it goes. Mouthful after glorious mouthful. I'm in hot, sweet, salt, sour heaven, with an ice-cold Tiger beer to break my sweat.

God, that's good. The deities above my head must be on the job. This is your typical old Hanoi house– French colonial with Asian customization – the latter bits and bobs a testament to the poorer years of communism and of making ends meet; a charming cultural mish-mash of past and present. And that's Hanoi all over: it's where coolie-hatted cyclists also ride motorbikes; baguettes are found alongside noodles; an opera house, sparkling like Versailles, sits alongside stove-and-stool outdoor kitchens; roast dog is next to pet dog; and the dollar meets the dong. The food markets hold charming chaos too, and I head for Hang Da for a plunge.

Shoppers, traders and fruit-laden traffic cram the makeshift alleys. Scooters jostle alongside hawkers with baskets of gleaming green swamp spinach; stalls creak under the weight of piles of Schiaparelli-pink dragon fruit; women squat over buckets of edible aquaria – rows of pink and blue plastic washing-up bowls, glass tanks and paddling-pool-sized tubs alive and kicking with eels, catfish, lungfish, ginormous snails, prawns and angry crabs with pincers bound. We've had a downpour and the polythene bags of dried shrimp, vermicelli and lots of unidentifiable desiccated things now dangle and drip. I buy a blue disposable bag mac. Bad idea. I should have avoided the coloured one, as the boil-in-the-bag effect leeches colour, and I turn out blue.

You can grab a bite at the markets too. Much is Western-mouth friendly, less zoological and more scoffable. Start with the banh cuon, freshly steamed rice pancakes rolled up with chopped mushroom and white radish, served at the side of the Hang Da in a white-tiled hall full of open kitchens and slim benches. The delicate parcels should be sprinkled with pounded dried shrimp and crispy shreds of garlic; fellow diners will pull selectively at the herbs and leaves in the little bowls dotted along the table, and

spoon on nuoc cham (a thin chilli dipping sauce flavoured with lime and fish sauce). For the next course, move in further amid the clatter and scrape of tin bowl, and the squawk, chop, thud, crack and slice of fowl and veg on block. I'd choose the com rang thap cam (egg fried rice, stuck with anise sausage, green beans, pickled cabbage and chicken) then enjoy it amid the furore of steam and smoke. Everyone scoffs with blind concentration, oblivious to the adjacent squawks of butchery.

But if it's breakfast you're after – say, after a dawn trip to the flower market (beside Nghi Tam Avenue) – then breakfast pho (thin ribbon rice noodles) is de rigueur had from one of Hanoi's old street kitchens: hole-in-the-wall set-ups, crowded with vast pots of steaming stock, fragrant and bubbling with pork bones. On the pavement, sat under a tarpaulin on a doll's-house-sized stool, you'll encounter a bowl of pure comfort food: starchy noodles with chicken or beef in hot broth. It's inhaling food, aromatic and blastingly fresh, yet based on thrift, so meat is minimal. For a few dong more, an egg yolk can be plopped in - plus there's the usual little bowls of herbs, beansprouts, pickles and chilli vinegars to play with ∎

3 days in Hanoi

No-one is about in the backstreets of antique Hué, yet ritual fires to the dead flare up here and there in the dark. Little fold-out tables massed with photos and food bits for the long-gone offer peace in a haze of joss-stick smoke: effects of memory, end and beginning for those gone in the Tet Offensive of 1968. On one verandah, where birdcages hang, is Ong Tao, a house-turned-evening-restaurant, next to a pond that throbs with bull frog and insect. They fall silent on approach, like someone's turns off the tropical atmosphere's CD or something, then presses 'play' as soon as you pass. I eat alone, happily digging into a refreshing shrimp cucumber salad; a plate of sticky chicken, donated by some lean but tasty bird; and 'dipping squid', a Vietnamese fondue-cum-hotpot, a broth afloat with a swirly-carpet of pineapple and garlic chive, with a platter of raw squid for poaching – booby-trapped with dangerously small chillies, armed to nuke lips and tongue.

Duong Han Thuyen, a leafy street in the Imperial Enclosure of the 'Forbidden Purple City', is another night-time spot. As dusk falls, soup kitchens move in, tarpaulins are strung up, and along the pavements under the trees, oil lamps twinkle against the black. Pots bubble and bump with stock, vapours snake and waft, and chatter is hushed and muffled, as if heard through the canvas of a campsite. Everyone sells the same: thick round wheat noodles in broth with quails' eggs, a sliver of meat and a handful of chive and roushong leaves (a mint) for 5,000 dong a bowl. 20p. I'd planted myself at a Mr Hoang's tables, for his smile and his fat tummy read right. His sister doled out the soup, while he jollied about like a Hobbit, bringing me banana leaf parcels, precisely folded, tied and cute, with raw garlic – and a cold Huda beer. One of the parcels is nem (fermented pressed pork with chilli) and the other cha (similar but with more peppery bite). Like a French saucisson, in fact. I have another pair, another and another.

They're very good, and soon my feet are gone to a pile of banana leaf litter.

Merrily Mr Hoang gets up and down, round face, busying and fumbling in his pockets. Then chuckling he brings little cakes of peanut and sesame paste, plus some of his home-made brew, a thimbleful of rice and ginseng wine. Then yet more nem and cha with green tea, and he's gotten very excitable – any minute now and I reckon he'll somersault like a Bilbo Baggins and disappear. Next day, he and the soup stalls have vanished. Not a wisp of noodle to let on, just a green-shaded Hué street ∎

Forbidden purple city

as dusk falls, soup kitchens move in

Cao lau noodles

Vietnam **177**

Noodles with soy-simmered pork and herbs are the star in Hoi An's culinary crown. A gorgeous thing, found nowhere else but in this antique town. The noodles are made from rice that has been soaked with ash in calcium-rich water, which makes them extra elastic. The croûtons that top the lot evolved from thrift, as once they were made from the left-over gunk from peanut oil production, but are now made from left-over rice noodles – pork scratchings work well too. Thrift has a ton of good things to answer for in Vietnamese food. Back home I use regular rice noodles to make this. Serve with dinky bowls of rice vinegar floated with sliced chilli, for sprinkling over before eating. (See left).

350g boneless and skinless pork loin
salt and black pepper
1/2 tsp ground star anise
1/2 tsp ground cinnamon
1 stick lemongrass, trimmed and finely chopped
1 birdseye chilli, finely sliced
2 tsp caster sugar
groundnut oil
1 tbsp fish sauce
100ml soy sauce
200g round rice noodles (bun) or other noodles
3 handfuls beansprouts
4 handfuls aromatic herbs (mint, basil,
  coriander, chopped garlic chives)
4 wide strips dried rice noodles, deep-fried
  until crisp and crumbled, or pork scratchings

Rub the pork loin with salt, pepper, star anise, cinnamon, lemongrass, chilli and sugar, then fry it in a drop of oil in a pan until it's lightly caramelized on all sides. Pour in the fish sauce and let this sizzle up around it, then pour in the soy sauce and 100ml water. Gently simmer, turning the pork occasionally, for about 10 minutes, or until just cooked through. Leave to cool in its sauce, drain, then slice – reserving any soy gravy for serving. It's fine if the meat and sauce are at room temperature on serving. Meanwhile, prepare the noodles according to their packet, then drain and refresh in cold water. To serve, dunk the softened noodles into a panful of boiling water to reheat, along with the beansprouts so they wilt. Pile these into four bowls, top with the sliced pork, then pile on the herbs, crispy noodle crumbs or pork scratchings, and dress with any remaining pork-soy gravy.

Dipping squid hotpot

A Vietnamese fondue-cum-Mongolian hotpot. Use fine slivers of tender beef steak if you're nonplussed by squid. You could just ladle this all out as a soup.

2 medium-sized prepared and cleaned
  squid, cut into rings
4 hot red chillies, finely chopped
a handful of coriander leaves
4 small shallots, sliced
2 tbsp vegetable oil
2 tomatoes, quartered and deseeded
handful of fresh pineapple slices,
  quartered
4 tbsp rice vinegar
2 sticks lemongrass, trimmed and smashed
handful of canned bamboo shoots or
  fresh beansprouts
1 baby leek or 2 spring onions, sliced
2 tbsp caster sugar
salt
fish sauce

Lay the squid on a plate and sprinkle with a little chopped chilli and some coriander leaves. Gently fry the shallots and half the remaining chopped chilli in the oil without browning, then stir in the tomatoes and pineapple and fry for a minute or so more. Stir in the vinegar, lemongrass, bamboo shoots, leek, caster sugar and a litre of water, and season well with salt and fish sauce. Let this bubble for a good 5 minutes. Pour into a fondue pan or steamboat hotpot set on the table, with its fuel and flame. Using chopsticks, add some squid to the simmering pot, letting it cook for a minute or so. Ladle back into a small bowl, with a little of the broth and its goodies (minus the lemongrass). Pile on coriander and the remaining chilli, and eat.

Green leaf soup

Leaf soups are the lightest of broths, and are often made with water – for the flavour is about green things. You could use a very light chicken or pork stock. Prawns can be popped in too. A spot-on counter-balancer to the rich. Burma likes this too, though a bitter edge from a lemony herb and a dab of MSG would be dropped in.

2cm piece white radish (mooli), finely sliced (optional)
2 spring onions or some garlic chives, chopped
2 good handfuls Asian cabbage leaves, such as water spinach or choi-sum
handful of shreds of white cabbage or Chinese leaves
salt and MSG (optional)
good pinch of caster sugar
handful of coriander leaves and stems, roughly chopped

Heat 1.5 litres water in a pan, and chuck in everything but the coriander, seasoning it extra well. Give it a taste. Allow the greens to wilt for about 3 minutes, then chuck in the coriander and serve.

Cha Ca La Vong noodles

This is a beauty, now a classic, and one that you should really know. Everything is set out on the table, then each person chopsticks some noodles into their bowl, piles on the dilled fish, herb leaves and some peanuts and then spills over a little nuoc cham. If you're non-plussed about the DIY scheme of things, serve it all assembled in bowls. (See left).

Pound together the garlic, galangal and turmeric to make a paste – or crush and finely grate, then mix together. Toss the fish with the fish sauce, a touch of salt, some pepper, the chilli and sugar, then toss through the paste, until the fish is evenly coated and leave, covered and refrigerated, for a good 2 hours or overnight.

Heat a heavy frying pan – something cast-iron is just the job – until smoking hot, then pour in about 2 tbsp oil. Pile in the fish. Allow to sizzle and splutter for about 2 minutes before turning the pieces over, then fry for a further minute. Add about 3 tbsp water, bubble up, then chuck all the dill on top and fold through – it should wilt but not go completely floppy. Ideally, you want to take the hot pan to the table (sit it on a thick mat) and let everyone take what they want, when they want it. The remaining ingredients should all have been piled into bowls and set out on the table.

3 fat cloves garlic
4cm piece fresh galangal or root ginger, peeled
4cm fresh turmeric root or 2 tsp ground turmeric
500g firm white fish fillet (conger eel, monkfish, pollack, whiting), skinned and cut into chunks
2 tsp fish sauce
salt and black pepper
pinch of ground chilli
1/2 tsp caster sugar
vegetable oil
2 very big bunches of dill, roughly chopped

To serve

4 spring onions, each sliced into 4
300g vermicelli noodles, cooked, drained and rinsed, according to the packet's instructions
4 tbsp lightly crushed toasted peanuts (see page 236)
nuoc cham (see page 180)
handful each of mint and basil leaves

Crispy spring rolls

Wood-ear mushrooms can join the mix: a dried brown fungus (had from Oriental stores) that needs a soak in water to soften before being chopped up. Totally optional here, but add a few to the stuffing if you have them. Nuoc cham dipping sauce (see below) is a must on wolfing; a wrapper's delight. (See right).

12 small rice paper sheets
vegetable oil
handful of fragrant herbs and salad leaves
nuoc cham (see below)

Filling
25g dried rice vermicelli noodles
300g minced pork or prawns
salt and black pepper
3 small shallots, finely chopped
1 clove garlic, crushed
2 tsp fish sauce
pinch of caster sugar
4 spring onions, chopped
a handful of beansprouts, chopped
1/2 medium carrot, grated
1 small free-range egg white

Dipping sauce
Nuoc cham

The classic dipping sauce found on every Vietnamese table. You can change the sauce to suit: add grated ginger, shredded carrot or white radish (mooli); use all lime juice and no vinegar; go more pungently Vietnamese and beat in a teaspoon of toasted shrimp paste; and for a milder sauce, stir in 2 tbsp water or coconut water – ideal for the dipping sauce to rice-paper-wrapped rolls. Makes a fab oil-free (= fat-free) salad dressing too.

2 cloves garlic, crushed
2 yellow or red birdseye chillies,
  sliced
2 tbsp caster sugar
2 tbsp lime juice
3 tbsp fish sauce (nuoc mam)
3 tbsp rice vinegar

Mix together all the ingredients and stir until the sugar has fully dissolved, then leave to stand for about 30 minutes before using.

For the filling, submerge the rice noodles in warm water until they turn soft, then drain them and chop them up. Mix the noodles with the remaining filling ingredients until thoroughly combined. Briefly dunk a rice paper in a plate of warm water and lift straight out and lay on a board – it will soften after a few seconds as it sits, without becoming too soft. Fold up one edge, then lay some of the prepared filling on this, compacting into a neat rectangular shape. Fold in both sides and roll up firmly to make a small and neat sausage-shaped parcel, maximum 2cm thick. Don't roll them too tightly, as the parcels could split when fried. Line them up on a plate as you go and keep them covered with clingfilm. They'll keep like this in the fridge for a few hours, until you want to fry them. Heat about a 4cm depth of oil in a wok or deep frying pan, then fry the parcels a few at a time until golden all over – making sure they don't touch each other as they fry. Drain on kitchen roll and keep them warm in the oven. To eat, wrap the rolls in herbs and then a lettuce leaf. Scoff while still hot, dunking each mouthful into the dipping sauce.

Chicken and mint salad

This salad relishes a wait, for the dressing deliciously pickles all the veg and boots up the chicken – making it excellent prep-ahead fuss-free stuff for friends who are programmed to be late. Poached chicken is the thing to use here; there again, it's great for hoovering up the remains of a roast.

1/4 crisp white cabbage, finely shredded
3 tbsp fish sauce
1 tbsp caster sugar
3 tbsp lime juice
black pepper
1 small cooked chicken or 4 cooked chicken breasts
3 long mild red chillies, deseeded and finely
  shredded
1 large carrot, finely shredded
big handful of mint leaves, shredded
3 tbsp toasted crushed peanuts (see page 236)
4 fat cloves garlic, finely sliced and fried
  until golden

Toss the cabbage with the fish sauce, sugar, lime juice and a few twists of pepper. Flake the meat into small chunks, then toss this with the cabbage mixture, with the shredded chillies and carrot. Leave on one side for an hour so the flavours mingle. Just before serving, toss through the mint, then pile on to plates and top with the peanuts and garlic.

Fellow diners pull selectively at herbs
and leaves.

Hanoi chicken noodle soup

Pho is Hanoi's breakfast soup. When made with slivers of beef it's called pho bo, and when with chicken, pho ga. An egg yolk can be popped in just before serving. Pile it into bowls and go mad on the alongside-condiment front: herbs, sprinklings and dippy things (coriander, fish sauce, chilli sauce, rice vinegar with chilli rings in, lime wedges etc.), that you weave into your bowl as you eat. Again, any cooked Sunday lunch chicken carcass and its attached clingage can be used to make this. Beef or pork bones can be used instead, with fine slices of sirloin beef added on serving.

1 x free-range poussin chicken or
  2 chicken legs or cooked carcass
1 bunch spring onions, trimmed
3cm piece fresh root ginger, peeled
  and thickly sliced
2 cloves garlic
2 whole star anise
1 cinnamon stick
2 tbsp whole dried shrimp
3 baby leeks, chopped (optional)
2 tbsp fish sauce
1 tbsp lime juice
salt and black pepper
400g dried thread or ribbon rice
  noodles (pho), cooked according to
  the packet's instructions

Put the chicken, half the spring onions and the next five ingredients into a large saucepan and cover with lightly salted water. Bring to a boil, skim off any flotsam, cover, and simmer very gently for about 25 minutes, then allow all to cool for about 20 minutes. Lift the chicken from the stock on to a plate. Strain the stock through a fine-meshed sieve and discard all the flavouring ingredients. Discard the chicken skin, pull the meat from the bones, and return the flaked chicken to the strained stock. Chuck in the leeks and heat through for about 5 minutes. Season with fish sauce, lime juice and pepper. Add more salt if needed. To serve, put a mound of cooked noodles in each bowl, add the remaining spring onion, and pour over the piping hot chicken soup. Eat with all the leafage, bits and pieces mentioned in the introduction, with chopsticks, spoons and fingers.

Caramel pork and prawns with pickled greens

Surf 'n' turf happens the world over. It's popular too in Hué's Hang Da morning market, where the indoor kitchens serve this topped with fried niblets of weeny salt-preserved fish and a dish of pickled vegetables alongside. The sweet, the crunchy and the bland, with the salted tartness of the preserved. Balance is all in Vietnam – and they're brilliant at it. If your thrust is for authenticity, then top the dish with some deep-fried salt-preserved dried fish – south-east Asian stores stock them vac-packed in small plastic bags.

5 tbsp caster sugar
3 tbsp fish sauce
3 shallots, sliced
3cm piece fresh root ginger, peeled and grated
salt and black pepper
1/4 head Chinese greens, cut into sections
4 tbsp rice vinegar
300g belly pork (with fat), sliced into
  bite-sized chunks
8 raw shell-on whole tiger prawns

Tip 4 tbsp of the sugar into a small saucepan, then gently melt over a medium heat, tipping the pan around a little. Keep heating until it turns a good caramel colour, then, standing back to avoid splutters, pour in the fish sauce, stir through and bubble for a few minutes. Stir in the shallots, grated ginger and some pepper and leave to thoroughly cool.

Pack the sliced greens into a small bowl or jar. Mix the remaining 1 tbsp sugar with the rice vinegar and 2 tbsp water and bring to a bubble, then pour over the greens and leave to cool.

Tip the pork into the cool caramel sauce and bring to a bubble, then turn the heat to very low and gently stew for 40 minutes. Add the prawns to the pork for the final 15 minutes of cooking and stir through to coat. Keep an eye on it so it doesn't catch and burn. Add a tbsp or two of water if things start to look too sticky and dry. Serve piled on to bowls of rice with the pickled greens alongside.

Smoky aubergine with coriander and chilli

Ideally, grill-roast the aubergine whole over charcoal. However, the oven is more convenient, so do roast if you wish. Deep-frying, chargrilling slices or steaming chunks all work beautifully – just stick on that dressing and it's delicious.

```
2 tbsp groundnut oil
1 dried red chilli, crumbled, or 1 tsp chilli flakes
2 fat cloves garlic, finely chopped
4cm piece fresh root ginger, peeled and grated
  (keep the juice too)
1 tbsp dark soy sauce
1 tbsp fish sauce
1 tbsp rice vinegar
1 tbsp caster sugar
1 tbsp lime juice
2 red chillies, sliced into rings
1 large aubergine or 4 long narrow violet
  aubergines, trimmed
2 tsp sesame oil
medium bunch of coriander, chopped
```

Gently heat the groundnut oil with the dried chilli, garlic and ginger without browning. Stir in the soy sauce, fish sauce and about 3 tbsp water and bubble up for a minute. In a separate bowl, mix the vinegar with the sugar, lime juice and sliced fresh chillies and leave on one side.

Roast the aubergines whole in a 190°C/375°F/Gas 5 oven until tender right through – or grill, steam or fry. Timing will depend on the thickness of the aubergines used (pierce with a knife; they should feel velvety soft).

Peel off and discard the aubergine skin, then cut the flesh into chunks and tumble with the reheated chilli ginger sauce, chilli vinegar and sesame oil. Lavish with coriander. Fabulous.

Sticky ginger chicken wings with herbs

Don't angst over the recherché-sounding herbs – anything sharp and fresh works well.

```
500g free-range chicken wings, halved
3 tbsp groundnut or vegetable oil
3 shallots, finely chopped
3 tbsp caster sugar
3 tbsp fish sauce
3cm piece fresh root ginger, shredded
1/2 tsp freshly ground black pepper
generous handful of herbs (eg perilla
  leaves, shiso cress, Thai basil or mint)
```

Fry the chicken in the oil in batches until lightly browned and slightly crisped at the edges. Remove and keep to one side. Add the shallots to the pan and soften in the oil, then add the sugar and gently cook until the mixture turns a rich-brown colour. Watch it doesn't burn. Pour in the fish sauce and stir. Add the fried chicken, ginger and pepper, cover and cook for 20–30 minutes, turning occasionally, until the liquid is a gloopy syrup and the chicken is caramelized, chewy-crispy and cooked. Serve in bowls stacked with herb leaves and plain boiled rice.

Hué prawn and cucumber salad

Strips of Vietnamese sausage (nem) were added at Hue's Ong Tao restaurant. Slices of Italian mortadella sausage, cut into strips, would be a near substitute. (See page 186).

```
16 cooked large prawns, halved lengthways
salt and black pepper
3 tbsp nuoc cham (see page 180)
1/2 cucumber, shredded
2 medium carrots, finely shredded
good handful of mint and coriander leaves
2 tbsp finely sliced shallots
```

Toss the prawns in a little salt and pepper and the nuoc cham and refrigerate for about 30 minutes. Lightly salt the cucumber and leave on one side for 30 minutes too, then rinse in cold water and drain. Add all the ingredients to the prawn mixture and toss through, keeping the shallots to sprinkle on top.

HUÉ PRAWN AND CUCUMBER SALAD, PAGE 185

lime and chilli butter clams with baguette

Freshness, beyond. A chilli meets butter meets citrus meets seafood simplicity. Home-grown fusion; my kinda food. A bivalve heaven I whipped from the Nam Seafood Restaurant, found on the beach road from Hoi An. (See left).

2 tsp ground pepper
2 tsp salt
juice of 1 lime
60g butter
1/2 tbsp coarse chilli paste
1kg large clams, scrubbed
baguette, to mop up the juices

Mix the pepper with the salt in a small dish, then add the lime juice. Mash the butter with the chilli paste. Set the clams across a grill rack and place over the coals of a fierce barbecue and grill until they pop open. Alternatively, scatter them across a heavy wide frying pan, put a lid on top, and bake over a high heat until they pop open. Discard any clams that do not open. Dab each clam body with the chilli butter and arrange over a big platter — the baking hot shells will keep them warm. To eat, spoon a drop of the lime pepper into each chilli-buttered clam, and suck the lot from the shell. Mop up all the lovely juices with baguette.

Banana leaf grilled mackerel

If you can't get banana leaves, wrap the fish parcel in foil instead. Eat with rice. Fail-safe barbecuable food.

small handful of rice vermicelli noodles
1 tbsp dried black Chinese mushrooms (optional)
250g skinned and boned mackerel (or tuna fillet),
  cut into very small chunks
1 tsp fish sauce
salt and black pepper
pinch of ground chilli
1/4 tsp ground turmeric
1/2 tsp caster sugar
1 fat garlic clove, crushed
2 spring onions, finely chopped
2 tsp vegetable oil
1/2 deribbed banana leaf, cut into 4 large squares
handful each of mint and basil leaves

Soak the noodles and mushrooms (if using) in cold water until just soft — about 10 minutes — then drain. Finely shred the mushrooms and roughly chop the noodles. Toss the chopped fish flesh with the fish sauce, salt, pepper, chilli, turmeric and sugar, then toss through the garlic, onions and oil. Fold through the prepared mushrooms and noodle. Place the mixture in the middle of a large square of banana leaf, then fold in the sides and wrap into a neat flat-looking square parcel. Lay this in the middle of a second piece of banana leaf and wrap up again. Repeat with the remaining leaves, to make a neat package. Grill the package over hot charcoal for about 6 minutes on each side; alternatively steam for about 10 minutes. Serve the contents of the parcel over steam-boiled rice (see page 236) and mound with herbs. Have dipping sauce (see page 180) at the ready.

Barbecue beef with starfruit Banh cuon

In Hoi An, cooked beef is rolled up in rice papers with slivers of starfruit, plantain and herbs to make banh cuon (summer rolls). Banh cuon sellers make their own rice papers from a rice flour paste, gracefully swirling the batter across muslin that is tied taut-as-a-drum across a steamer. We don't have the time or skill for such fiddle, so use instant rice paper wrappers instead: dunk rice papers in a dish of warm water for a few seconds and then leave on a tea-towel until they go limp. Arrange strips of cooked meat on top with slivers of starfruit (and possibly some plantain), plus herbs, turn in the edges to overlap the stuffing, then roll up tightly, and cut in half to serve, dunking each mouthful in nuoc cham dipping sauce. Or do as I suggest below. (See page 183).

1 stick lemongrass, trimmed and very
  finely chopped
2 small shallots, roughly chopped
3cm piece fresh galangal or root
  ginger, peeled and chopped
2 cloves garlic
pinch of five-spice powder
salt and black pepper
2 tsp caster sugar
2 tbsp fish sauce
1 large fillet steak or boneless pork
  steak, thinly sliced into strips
1 tbsp vegetable oil
1 tbsp runny honey

To serve
1 starfruit, shredded into thin strips
a handful of fragrant herbs, such as
  mint and basil
nuoc cham (see page 180)

In a mortar or processor, pound or blend together the lemongrass, shallots, galangal, garlic and five-spice powder with a smidgen of salt and some pepper to make a coarse paste. Mash in the sugar and 1 tbsp of the fish sauce. Tumble this with the sliced meat until it is well coated. Leave to bathe overnight or for as long as possible.

Just before grilling, add the oil and stir through to coat. Mix the remaining 1 tbsp fish sauce with the honey in a small bowl. Thread the strips of prepared meat lengthways on to skewers (so the meat lays out flat), then brush with the honey mixture and briefly grill over or under a fierce heat, turning once, until the meat is cooked and caramelized on both sides. Charcoal will give the most authentic flavour. Eat with strips of starfruit, herbs and nuoc cham dipping sauce, or with rice vermicelli and a sprinkle of toasted crushed peanuts.

Ginger squid salad

Vietnamese scoop this up with banh da, a toasted rice cracker – a poppadum lookalike – that puffs out when held over hot coals. Remember to soak the onion, as unsoaked raw onion will be way too powerful and you'll end up in tears. The secret to getting shallots crisp is to slice them well beforehand and then leave them spread out to dry a little, then slow-fry them with a dash of salt. Handy bags of ready-made crispy shallots can be bought from Oriental stores. (See right).

1 large very mild onion or 6 shallots
1-2 large squid (about 500g), cleaned and prepared
2 tbsp rice vinegar
3cm piece fresh root ginger, peeled
2 red chillies, deseeded and very finely chopped
  until pulped
3 tbsp nuoc cham (see page 180)
good big bunch of basil (preferably Thai)
4 good tbsp toasted crushed peanuts (see page 236)
3 tbsp crispy sliced shallots

The night before, finely slice the onion or shallots into long slender petal-shaped pieces, then put in a bowl of cold water and leave covered and refrigerated to extract the oniony punch. Drain well before using. Cut the squid body open and lay it out flat, then make diagonal score marks across it. Drop it into a pan of boiling water, adding the rice vinegar, and gently bubble for about 15 minutes, or until tender (and past the rubbery stage). Drain and finely slice the flesh, knife blade angled, so you end up with slivers that look a bit like coconut shavings. Pound or grate the ginger with the chillies to make a paste. Toss the squid with the drained onion and the nuoc cham, then toss with the herbs and pile into bowls, blobbing over the ginger paste. Heavily rain with toasted crushed peanuts and crispy shallots.

Singapore

billowing smells roll, like breakers, into the street

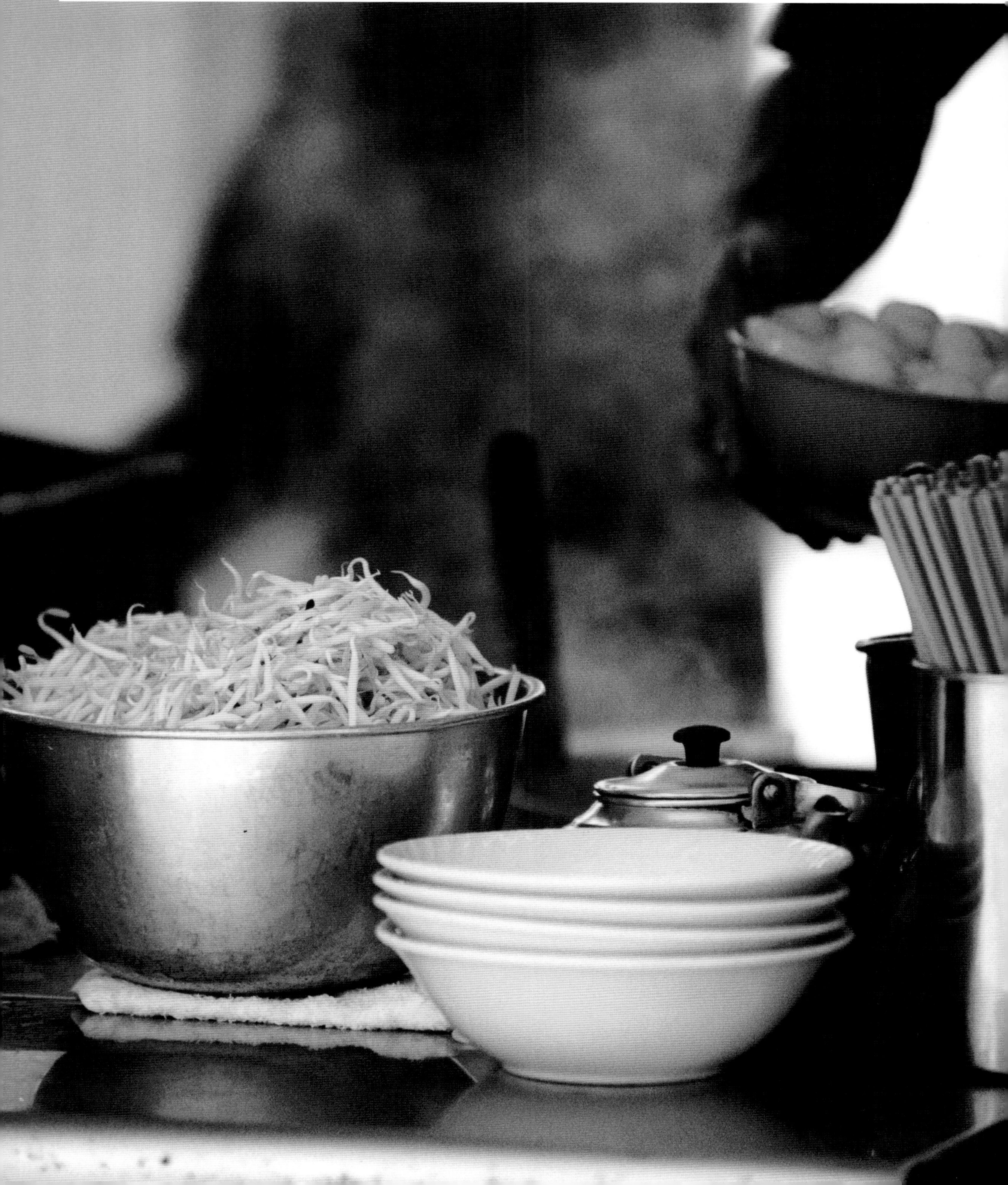

Singapore
flavours

Singapore is the smallest of all the Asian countries. It's Asia's roundabout, crossroads and underpass to the world. It's where concrete and glass meet bamboo and paper; businessman, foodstall hawker; Hindu, Buddhist; curry leaf, pandan leaf. And its food is a melting pot derived from all who surround – and pass through – it. Singapore is the grand-daddy of fusion food. Multicultural and multiracial, it's a melting-pot cuisine of Chinese, Malay, Indonesian and Indian: Asia's glorified wok. Singaporeans have blended Malay cooking with Chinese: the oomph of South-Asian shrimp paste and tamarind flavours buddies-up with the bland, thin, clear saucings of Southern Cantonese and Hokkien, known as Nonya cuisine. Yet the Chinese influence also remains in all its unadulterated glory. Indonesia and India join hands with their curries, satay and coconut-sauced things. Curries and satays are flavoured with rempah, a Nonya spice paste of pounded lemongrass, nuts, ginger or galangal, garlic, shallots, chillies, cumin, coriander, cinnamon, sugar and salt. And Singapore noodles. What are they? Every take-away in every land has its own version, for nowhere does noodles more varied than Singapore.

亞老

魚圓粿條

FISH BALL NOODLE

fish ball

Sapiah Ahmet, my cultural attaché for a day, is to meet me in the hotel lobby. Half expecting a sylph-like, small, suited Oriental with a china-doll face and no appetite, I meet a cuddly being in Muslim head-wrap who, by her lovely curvy shape, shoe-horned into Burberry mules, I'd judge loves food. We set off to trawl markets for all the foodstuffs we can put away. Sapiah is a fount of knowledge and doesn't stop. A sweetie who mothers me all day: 'Eat that, and that, finish it up now...' Bowls, platters, plates, cups and packets are fed my way in never-ending succession.

For kick-off, we dim sum in Chinatown's Smith Street. On a stainless-steel counter, open to the street, sits a mini Singapore skyline of creaking basket steamers. Trays and woven lids huff-and-puff with steam, sodden, soft and impregnated by the shrimp, pork, sesame and lotus of a thousand dim sum dinners. The billowing smells roll, like invisible breakers, into the street, seasoning all that pass. I'm sold. I buy. I'm at the counter before you can say duck-rice. I defy anyone to pass. There's a big chart on the white-tiled wall behind, divided into a grid, and each box has a number and a picture of three primped and crimped dumplings sat in their steaming trays. You point at what you want, and a lady as skinny as a chicken's claw looks blankly at you without a smile, but then gets you exactly what you want. It's an agonizing decision, what not to have, which fails to amuse Ms Chicken-foot. I back-track, she lifts the lids on everything yet again. A small cup-shaped tin of Chinese sausage and chicken sticky rice is turned out on to a plate, all glutinous and glistening, and is

brought to the table, followed by sweet pork buns, virgin-white dough balls stained with jammy trickles, black bean ribs in their requisite puddle of rendered fat and soy, and fish and pork balls in won-ton jackets, sucked tight. Plus the obligatory pot of jasmine tea. Dumped unceremoniously, you just know they're going to taste fab. Chopsticks drawn, chilli-shrimp oil on the mark, and I'm in. Sapiah elbowed-out on the sidelines.

And then we head west to Katong's Joo Chiat Road, to what was once a quiet seaside village, where old colonial villas are mixed with Peranakan-style terraces and Malay bungalows. The place for Straits-born Malay-Chinese fare. Tin Yeang restaurant, half-way down, is a big covered food court, all open to the streets with a line-up of madly busy and shouting shiny kitchens, each waving its own thing. Lit-up numbered pictures are their menus, and tables are shared in one big, light eating hall, where everyone is blasted by a wind-farm of pillar-mounted, cyclone-strength fans. Without them we'd all wilt in seconds.

A Peranakan lady with dyed-black thinning hair, volumized into big hair, totters to my table with something steaming. With painted-on eyebrows and a pyjama suit, mounted on heeled slip-ons tapering to genie-of-the-lamp up-turned snouts, she looks like she's up for an audition in Aladdin. Devouring her noodles like it's her last meal, she then gets up immediately and totters off. I eat laksa, a deep bowl of round rice noodles wallowing in a delicious great-grey-greasy river of coconut curried soup, inhabited by a myriad tiny

dried shrimp and snipped weed. Three large prawns, spliced lengthways, white flesh framed by pink, sit on top with strips of bendy sponge-like fried beancurd, gloriously drunk with coconut broth.

Back in Chinatown, frog porridge (a form of rice congee dimpled with frog meat) is on offer. Frogs in porridge are no man's land to me, and so I plump for fish ball noodle at Kuan's restaurant. It's an open-to-the-street, wipe-down-tile place with plastic everything, and the usual unforgiving neon. An old lady in a floral-patterned trouser suit, with eye-bags as puffed as her fish balls, busies around with a cloth, wiping spillages, as does a man of equal years with janitor's fingers. They have a dance that revolves around buckets: a bucket for dunking dirty chopsticks, buckets for rinsing, buckets for stock and water, and buckets holding chopped spring onions, noodles, fish balls and things. They work alongside a man juggling beansprouts and noodles, and bring me a bowlful that bumps buoyant with white balls. With just the right squeak, spring and bland comfort, the fish balls are a dream.

I go back in the evening, and pick at a crab, axed into four. A soothing dressing of spring onion gloop floods its nether regions, its nooks and crannies, a swirling weed of egg strands marbles its severed back. Then roast duck and sea cucumber hotpot: braised sea creatures gelatinous hide aplenty (and tastes like you'd expect), and a guarded amount of roast duck, with shiitake, baby corn, carrot, leek and onion in larval-hot gravy. Vertebrate deliciosa meets invertebrate elastica. A textural thing. Bet this old sea slug never guessed he'd end up with a duck ∎

noodle

Dumped unceremoniously, you just

Chopsticks drawn, chilli-shrimp

DIM SUM MUSHROOMS, PAGE 205

know they're going to taste fab

oil on the mark, and I'm in

DIM SUM RIBS WITH SALTED BLACK BEANS, PAGE 205

Dim sum duck noodle soup

Where there's dim sum, there's duck soup to be had. The Chinese would use their special roast duck for this – I give you a to-do-at-home quick version: steam it, then roast it, and it tastes the part. Cook it well before. There again, you could buy a ready-cooked half portion of roast duck from your local take-out and settle with that. I would.

4 duck legs
3 tsp five-spice powder
salt
2 tbsp soy sauce
1 tbsp runny honey
2 tsp sesame oil
200g egg noodles or other noodles
1.5 litres Asian chicken stock (see
  page 236)
2 tbsp oyster or hoisin sauce
4 spring onions, chopped
1/4 iceberg lettuce, roughly sliced or
  a bunch of watercress

Rub each duck leg with the five-spice and some salt, then mix the soy with the honey and 1 tsp sesame oil and rub this all over the legs too. Tightly wrap each leg in clingfilm, then steam in a steamer for 35 minutes. Leave to cool. The duck can now be stored in its wrapping for two days in the fridge if you wish. Unwrap the legs, lay on a roasting tray, and roast in a 200°C/400°F/Gas 6 oven until crisped up – about 25 minutes. Once cooled a tad, shred the meat – or if you're a dab hand with the cleaver, chop it into chunks. Again, this can be done much earlier, as the soup stock will reheat all. When hungry, cook the noodles according to the packet, strain and keep on one side. Then heat the stock with the remaining sesame oil and the oyster sauce until bubbling. Divide the cooked noodles, spring onions, greenery and duck between four bowls, then ladle in the hot broth and serve.

Pork dumpling, aubergine and salt-fish hotpot

Put the ginger, bamboo shoots and 2 spring onions, roughly chopped, into a processor and blast until finely chopped. Add the prawns, 1 tbsp each soy sauce and rice wine, 1 level tbsp cornflour, 1 tsp salt and some pepper and blast again until roughly minced, then tip this over the pork mince and mix well. Form into uneven walnut-sized balls, cover, then chill until firmed. Mix the remaining cornflour with 3 tbsp water. Cut the aubergine into long-shaped chunks, then fry it in a pool of vegetable oil on all sides until it begins to turn gold, then shift the aubergine on to kitchen roll.

Drain off all but 1 tbsp of the oil, then fry the garlic without browning. Stir in the white parts of the spring onions, the remaining rice wine and soy sauce, the vinegar and oyster sauce, 350ml water and the cornflour mix, and bubble up for a minute, while stirring. Arrange the dumplings, aubergine, and sauce in a small casserole pan or Chinese sandpot, crumbling in the preserved fish as you go. Bring to a bubble, then cover, and cook on a lowish heat (or in a 190°C/375°F/Gas 5 oven) for 45 minutes. Serve lavished with the shredded spring onion tops – shredded fresh root ginger will put punch in too.

Acquired tastes are my kinda thing, and this is one: the salty, faintly pungent and fishy, with the bland, the velvet and the slippery. If salt-fish eludes you (it's an Asian shop thing), use salted anchovies instead – but not the olive oil canned one. (See page 206).

3cm piece fresh root ginger, peeled
  and shredded
2 tbsp canned bamboo shoots, drained
5 large spring onions, halved, green
  severed from white
250g cooked peeled prawns (defrosted
  ones are fine)
3 tbsp soy sauce
3 tbsp Chinese rice wine
3 tbsp cornflour
salt and pepper
250g fatty pork mince
1 aubergine
vegetable oil and sesame oil
3 fat cloves garlic, sliced
2 tbsp Chinese black or rice vinegar
2 tbsp oyster sauce
20g salt-preserved fish, or 2 salted
  anchovies, fried until crisp

Dim sum ribs with salted black beans

No stonking great ribs here, this is more about soupçons of dim sum flavour sucked from the skimpiest meat-hugging bone. Easy and delicious.

```
1 tsp salt
1 tbsp caster sugar
1 tbsp Chinese rice wine
1 tbsp soy sauce
2 tsp sesame oil
2 red chillies, chopped, plus some fine slices
2 cloves garlic, crushed
2 tbsp oyster sauce
2 tbsp salted black beans
300g spare ribs, cut across the bone into 4cm
  sections (get the butcher to do this)
1 red pepper, deseeded and cut into chunks
```

Combine all the ingredients except the spare ribs and red pepper in a bowl, toss the spare ribs in the mixture and leave overnight, covered and refrigerated, to bathe. Place them with their bath of flavours in a shallow dish set in a steaming tray, then steam for 20 minutes. Slip the red pepper pieces around the ribs in the steamer, carry on steaming for a further 5 minutes, or until cooked, then serve.

Roast pork and clam sticky rice

Up-front, no bullshit now. If you live in the sticks, don't attempt this, for you'll require a Chinatown on your doorstep for all the unusuals. I've put it in, for it's a cinch to cook, tastes glorious, and, more to the point, where would life go without some challenges and aspirational goals – seriously, where would it? Hard-to-get ingredients don't spell hard-to-make. And it's a good hoover-upper of roast leftovers.

```
400g Chinese sticky (glutinous) rice,
  soaked overnight
3 dry-cured Chinese sausages, thinly
  sliced
500g cooked sliced crispy pork or duck
  (from your local Chinese) or cooked
  duck or chicken
2 tbsp dried wood-ear mushrooms, soaked
  in water (optional)
500g clams, scrubbed and soaked in
  cold water
sesame oil
soy sauce or bottled chilli shrimp
  oil, to serve
```

Dim sum mushrooms

Dim sum at home can be easy; it's not all about tricksy dumpling making. Your best bet for dough-wrapped packages is to buy them from Asian stores, ready-made (frozen or fresh), then steam them with your own home-made things, and palm them off as your own.

```
salt and pepper
3cm piece fresh root ginger, peeled
2 cloves garlic, sliced
2 tbsp dark soy sauce
3 tsp sesame oil
1 tbsp vegetable oil
2 tbsp rice wine
12 fresh shiitake mushrooms
2 spring onions, halved crossways and
  green tops finely shredded
```

Combine all the ingredients except the mushrooms and green part of the spring onions in a bowl, then toss the mushrooms in the mixture until well coated. Tip the mushrooms, along with any collected liquids, on to a plate that will fit your steamer tray. Steam for 10 minutes and serve with the shredded spring onion.

Drain the soaked rice. Line a large steaming tray, or four individual bamboo steaming trays, with muslin. Spread over the rice, then scatter over the Chinese sausage and the pork, then steam over boiling water for 25 minutes. After 20 minutes of the cooking time, add the mushrooms and clams on top of the rice and sprinkle with sesame oil, then replace the lid and carry on steaming for about 4 minutes. The rice should be sticky and cooked and the clams opened (discard any that are still shut). Rake up the rice with all the bits and pieces, and serve in the steaming baskets. Season chopsticked mouthfuls with soy sauce or dip into chilli oil.

PORK DUMPLING, AUBERGINE AND SALT-FISH HOTPOT, PAGE 204

Wok mushrooms and greens

If using dried shiitake mushrooms, soak them in 250ml water first, discard their stems, and use their water with the cornflour.

Mix the soy sauce with 2 tbsp water and the cornflour, and keep to one side. In a wok, heat the oils together and stir-fry the mushrooms with salt and pepper until they're seared a little. Throw in the garlic, ginger and chillies and stir through, then add the vegetables and beansprouts. Stir-fry over a fierce heat for about 1 minute, adding a dash more seasoning. Pour in around 150ml water, bubble up for about 30 seconds, then stir in the cornflour mixture and the oyster sauce and bubble up to make a good gloopy sauce. Serve piled on to plates or in bowls, and sprinkle each serving with toasted sesame seeds.

2 tbsp soy sauce
1 tbsp cornflour
2 tbsp vegetable or sunflower oil
2 tsp sesame oil
16 shiitake mushrooms, thickly sliced
salt and pepper
3 cloves garlic, sliced lengthways
4cm fresh ginger, peeled and shredded
2 long red mild chillies, deseeded and
    shredded lengthways
6 spring onions, shredded
400g mangetout, sugar snaps, asparagus
    tips or sliced Chinese greens
handful of beansprouts
1 tbsp oyster sauce
4 tsp toasted sesame seeds, to serve

Braised duck rice plate

The duck is first poached, then roasted – and then the braising liquid makes gravy. Simple, and hugely effective.

1 whole duck
6 shallots, chopped
1 litre light chicken stock (fresh,
   instant or Asian stock on page 236)
500ml dark soy sauce
400ml Chinese rice wine
3 tbsp runny honey
2 tsp salt
4 star anise or 2 tsp ground star anise
vegetable oil
1 tbsp vegetable oil
1/2 head Chinese leaves, cut into
   chunks, or 4 heads bok choi
1 tbsp cornflour mixed with 2 tbsp water

To serve
Steam-boiled rice (see page 236)
small bunch of spring onions, shredded

Sit the duck, bottom up, in a colander in the sink, then pour over a kettleful of boiling water, aiming inside as well as out. Leave the duck to drain. Put all the remaining ingredients apart from the vegetable oil, Chinese leaves and

cornflour in a casserole pan (something in which the duck will snugly fit) and bring to a bubble, stirring to dissolve the honey. Then put in the duck, breast down, cover with a lid and gently braise on a very slow bubble for about 1 1/2 hours, topping up the water level if it drops below the duck and turning the duck over for the last 20 minutes. Once cooled, lift out, drain off the delicious gravy, then leave the duck covered in the fridge for a few hours or overnight. Refrigerate the gravy, then skim off the fat.

Rub the duck all over with a touch of oil, set it on a roasting tray and roast in a 200°C/400°F/Gas 6 oven for about 30 minutes, or until it is cooked through, polished brown and crisp. Cut out and discard the backbone, then cleave the two halves, bones and all, into manageable sections. Stir-fry the greens in a drop of hot duck fat or oil for a few seconds, add about 4 tbsp water, stir through, then let splutter for about 30 seconds. Stir in 100ml of the duck's braising gravy and the cornflour mixture and bubble for about a minute. Serve the duck and greens and thick gravy on the rice, scattered with shredded spring onion.

Nonya pot-braised chicken

One to bung in the oven and then forget about. Well almost...

1 small chicken, spatchcocked
salt
4 tbsp dark soy sauce
4 tbsp Chinese rice wine
1 tbsp caster sugar
vegetable oil
4 shallots, chopped
3cm piece fresh root ginger, peeled and shredded
2 hot red chillies
2 cloves garlic, crushed
4 young leeks or 4 large spring onions, shredded and washed

Rub the chicken with salt then pop in a strong bag (a freezer-type one), with the soy sauce, rice wine and sugar. Rub everything in by massaging the bag on the bird, and leave to bathe for a few hours or so. Remove the bird and its marinade from the bag, keeping all the juices to one side, then carefully fry all over in 2 tbsp oil in a casserole pot until golden looking. Add the shallots, ginger, chillies and garlic, tucking them around and allowing them to fry a little. Pour in the reserved marinade, add 4 tbsp water, bring to a bubble then cover and braise in a 180°C/350°F/Gas 4 oven for 1 hour. Remove the lid and turn up to 200°C/400°F/Gas 6, so that the bird browns a little. Stir-fry the leeks quickly in 1/2 tbsp oil, add to the pot and serve.

Black pepper crab with curry leaves

Chilli crab is Singapore's fave wokked mollusc, and comes in all guises. This one I unearthed in a food hall, and with a touch of India about its gills, it's gorgeous. Every nook, cranny and hollow yields the sweetest – sometimes meagre, sometimes generous – morsels. It's a slow-picking game, so the pleasure comes in little doses and spurts; hands-on stuff, which demands constant licking, so finger bowls and wipes at the ready, and that bowl of regular rice.

2 cooked mud crabs or blue-swimmer crabs (ask the fishmonger to remove the gills), or 8 cooked cold-water fat crab claws (in the shell)
3 long dried red chillies, deseeded and chopped
4 cloves garlic, finely chopped
4 tbsp groundnut oil
a knob of fresh root ginger, peeled and grated
1 tsp caster sugar
3 tsp coarsely crushed black pepper or chopped fresh peppercorns
15 curry leaves
1 tbsp fish sauce
2 tbsp sweet chilli sauce
1 tbsp Maggi sauce or dark soy sauce
1 bunch spring onions, very finely shredded

First remove the top shell from the crabs, then quarter them and, using a rolling pin, thwack the shell of the large front claws to smash it but leave it all intact. In a wok, fry the chillies and garlic in 2 tbsp of hot oil until the garlic starts to colour, then add the ginger, sugar, black pepper, curry leaves and remaining oil and fry until the leaves have darkened. Add the fish sauce and sweet chilli sauce and fry for 30 seconds more. Toss in all the bits of crab (including the top shells) and shunt and push the lot around in the wok, making sure everything gets well plastered in the richly flavoured oil – spoon some gunge and oil inside the carapaces too. Fry all over, tipping and turning all the parts until the sauce has really darkened and the crab is flecked with black; 3-4 minutes. Serve piled with spring onion. Implements of sorts, to wheedle out the claw meat, are in order.

Prawn chow mein

Textural heaven. The pancake of noodles goes deliciously squelchy in the middle, yet the perimeter stays crunchy.

300g dried egg noodles
12 peeled raw tiger prawns
salt and white pepper
1 free-range egg white
cornflour
1 tbsp caster sugar
1 tbsp black, or rice, vinegar
vegetable oil
3 cloves garlic, sliced
1/2 small head Chinese leaves,
  cut into chunks
4 spring onions, chopped into
  short lengths
handful of mangetout
handful of beansprouts

Soak the noodles in warm water for 15 minutes until they're softened a little. Drain them through a sieve, spread out over a tea-towel to dry a little, then arrange over a plate in a big flat nest shape. Toss the prawns with a mixture of salt, pepper, the egg white and 1 tbsp cornflour, and leave on one side. Mix 2 tbsp cornflour with 1 tsp salt, the caster sugar and vinegar and 6 tbsp cold water in a jug. Put all this by the hob.

Heat a deep pool of oil in a wok, then slip the noodle 'nest' into the oil and fry for a few seconds, until it's puffed up and crisped. Watch out for splatters. Lift it out, drain on kitchen roll, then tip out all but about 3 tbsp of the oil from the wok. Next, add the garlic and fry until it starts to take on a touch of colour, then add the prawns and stir-fry for about a minute, then tip in the sliced Chinese leaves, spring onions and mangetout, and stir-fry for another minute. Chuck in the beansprouts and toss through. Next, pour in the contents of the jug and bubble up, and mix through, cooking for a further minute. Put the crispy noodles on to a big plate, then spoon the contents of the wok over the top. Soy sauce and chopsticks at hand, and you're off.

Crab and sweetcorn soup

Monosodium glutamate features in every eat-out crab and sweetcorn soup, so there's no harm once-in-a-while in adding a dab when salting at home. In fact, its sodium levels are lower than that of our everyday table salt. I leave it with you.

350g fresh cooked white crab meat
2 tsp Chinese rice wine
salt
1 × 230g can creamed sweetcorn
1 litre Asian chicken stock (see
  pages 236)
2 tbsp cornflour mixed with 2 tbsp water
1 tsp vegetable oil
2 free-range egg whites
good handful each of coriander leaves
  and shredded spring onion

In a bowl, mix the crab meat with the rice wine and a small pinch of salt. Tip the creamed corn into a saucepan with the stock and bubble up, then stir in the crab mixture. Tip the cornflour mixture in next and stir it in. Allow to gently bubble until thickened, then stir in the oil and turn off the heat. Now taste, adding more salt if it needs it. Beat 1 tbsp water with the egg whites, then slowly pour into the soup while stirring. Ladle into bowls and thatch with some coriander leaves and shredded spring onion.

Bali

Bali
flavours

Bali is but one small island in the vast archipelago that is Indonesia. Yet, in culinary terms at least, it is the brightest waterlily in the Indonesian pond — a varied and veritable cast of thousands that includes the Malaku islands (formerly Moluccas), famed for their spice. Islands that have gone through the mill of invasion, occupation and cultural assimilations — including tourism. Yet life remains humble, contentedly jogging along with its deep-rooted respect for all that sustains it: the land, the air and the sea. The spice islands' plantations of clove, cinnamon and nutmeg, and the towering groves of kenari nut trees are no longer the trading commodity they used to be, yet they stand testimony to the Dutch occupation and still help sustain the population. Indonesia's food is one of those global melting-pots that's been left on the back-burner, on slow simmer, for centuries. Malay ancestry fused with Chinese, Indian, Dutch, Portuguese, Spanish, Arab traders, colonizers and local blood have all added their bit, and it's time that we in the West lifted the lid on this exotic pot and got stuck in. Staples and flavourings that crop up throughout the islands are: rice, chillies, coconut milk, kecap manis (a thick, rich, sweet soy sauce, and incidentally where we nabbed the word 'ketchup' from), shrimp paste (terasi), candlenuts (kemiri) and palm sugar. These are blended and balanced with other things. For every sour or salty flavour there's a counterbalance of sweetness; dishes blistering with chillies come with cool sliced fruits or something steeped in coconut milk. Flavourings come fresh, as opposed to powdered: leaves, roots, stems and fruits are chopped, smashed and pounded into pastes as and when they're needed. Sambals (coarsely chopped hot sauces) are served with many things and they're wokked with petai beans and eaten with curries — as are acar (pickles). Think Bali. Think green. Think acres of paddy fields. Contoured arrangements of dazzling cellulose-green steps colonize Bali's every available hillside. No prizes then for guessing that rice (in white, red and black) is the key staple. Paddies also support fish and float with happy Bali ducks (their droppings further nourishing the rice, frogs and eels) that end up hung, drawn and quartered at the markets. Plain boiled rice is the every-dayer, yet they get inventive with it too, flavouring it with coconut milk and pandanus leaf or lemongrass, or with shrimp paste and sambal, and then wokking it to make their golden oldie, nasi goreng. Rice is ritual; valued and respected, it's woven into the unique Bali-Hindu culture in tiny elegantly wrapped macramé-like parcels which are placed as offerings to the gods at doorways and temples to appease the demon spirits, Bhuta and Kala, and the blood-sucking goblins, witches and giants of the night. Blood and guts make up a true part of the Bali diet. Lawar is a coconut-chilli-shredded salad, its dressing — blood. Along with fried chicken, the tourists popularize mee goreng (stir-fried noodles) in all its variations. Numerous species of sea and freshwater fish are landed every morning and flogged from Jimbaran's open market or from baskets on the beach. Vanilla beans can be found growing in the volcanic mountains of Bali. Though most of the population is Muslim, Balinese Hindus eat pig, as do Torajans of Sulawesi, who go in for buffalo feasting at festive and funeral occasions. Buffalo are slaughtered in front of guests. Invited to stay for one such blood-bath, I declined after the first animal went down — and stuck with fish for the rest of my trip.

Still no plane has arrived. I wash one pair of pants and one T-shirt daily, patient. For after flying me from Ambon through cockroach hell – a critter-crawling ride sauced by the drip of air-con – the airline has forgotten, lost, or whatever, my bag. I sit now on top of a volcano, Gunung Api, on the rim of a crater, on the island of Bandaneira, perched on the map in the Banda Sea, feeling like the 'eensiest' speck on Earth, and can't imagine how anything, let alone the Calvins and Levis of this world, could ever reach me.

It's a tiny island, and this vast and gaping smouldering caldera hogs most of it. Like some British roadside picnicker, a hair's breadth away from the rampant jaws of death, I take time out on the sulphurous ashes: a towering cone that blew its top in 1988. In volcano years, that's a mere yesterday. One of the world's most active. A vomit of pumice spills like petrified porridge on my right, cutting a black and devilish scourge into the sea below. A reminder of recent bad temper. Bandaneira is one of the 13,000-plus volcanic islands that make up Indonesia, and the place to take in one of our planet's most rare vistas. A sea and sky of infinity spreads out before me, in a meld of Quink-ink blues; things glint and glitter, pin-pointing the far reaches.

To the north lies Ambon, where only yesterday I'd been doing sand-and-sea. Idling an afternoon away on a beach, eating boiled corn and sour fruit with some unfamiliar-looking roots smothered in hot peanut sauce. I'd sat on a bench in the shade of a strung-up piece of tarpaulin while a warung, this one a toothless crone as scourged as driftwood, pounded peanuts, palm sugar and chilli into a thick paste the colour of flotsam cork. Freshly sliced fruits and slivers of root were handed to me, plus bamboo cocktail sticks for spearing.

East of me lies Irian Jaya, New Guinea, and to the west, Sulawesi, a splatted starfish–shaped island, home to the Christian Toraja of Tonatoraja, and a 'witch' who 'dances naked with eggs under her breasts through the forests of the night'. The 'witch' cooked me a supper of fiddlehead ferns fried with tomato; shredded banana flower and black rice in coconut milk; grilled grouper sauced black with pamarassan (a black fruit paste) and pa' piong munuk; minced chicken and lemongrass, slow-roasted over a fire in bamboo – all moistened with blood – in her restaurant. The nearby pentecostal Christian-run Misiliana Hotel had branded restaurateur Sylvie Manley a 'witch', for she'd complained of their noise pollution: holiday camp-style religious broadcasts, loudspeakered through the hotel gardens, that filter into her neighbouring home. 'When a Child is Born' and 'When the Saints go Marching in' Hammond organs nightly in the Misiliana's cocktail bar, sinking every Toraja Sunrise. Sylvie is an American, married to a local Borneo man, and a canny businesswomen with a restaurant popular with travellers and now a hotel in the idyllic Togian islands.

Bali. Island of votive offerings, jungle temples, spirit houses, ceremonies, and elaborate festivals, lies to the south-east of me. Beautiful Bali, with its full-on Hindu culture. Brochures depict it brimming with picture-postcard honeymoon promise: the land of spiritual being, flower baths, zen-like spas spilling with soul-reaching unguents, swaying palm and I-love-you sunsets. Everyone with a flower pinned either behind their ear or in their cocktail, and a subservient smile. Move inland, north of Ubud, and the tourist tideline peters out and travellers' Bali begins.

A feast, known as a rijsttafel (a Dutch word, and invention, meaning rice table), is the greedy-pig way to eat Bali in one sitting. And I did, but for research purposes, at Ketut's, a by-appointment-only lunch place with garden bungalows, just beyond Ubud. The following may read like an inordinate amount to digest (and it is) – an utter maelstrom of everything ever picked and pounded (and it was) – yet it tastes gorgeous. Went something like this: duck, bebek batutu, stuffed with a fried bumbu (spice paste) of cassava leaves, nuts, shallots, garlic and chilli, wrapped in layers of banana leaves and interred within a fire of coconut husks; satay of chicken and coconut, a threaded kebab mix of meat pounded with jangkap (a seasoning of bitter hot salam leaves, galangal, wild ginger, turmeric root, nuts, shrimp paste, chilli, tamarind, palm sugar, cumin, lime juice and shallots); vegetable dishes got a lime-and-starfruit-leaf, nutmeg, cinnamon, cardamom and clove treatment; there was brem (a fermented rice wine) and nasi goreng (fried rice) to mop up with and then krupuk (ceremonial rice crackers), and fresh fruit and teh jahe (sweet ginger tea) to finish. Phew. Flop. Sleep. Don't pass go, don't collect...

A hum nears my volcano. It's a dive boat returning from the reef. My boatman is waiting and we paddle back across the sparkly bay to where the nutmeg groves tower around the old 1611 Dutch fort, Belgica. I dive that afternoon. Just over the way, at Banda Besa. A wall dive in virgin scuba territory, crystal-clear, free of the scars and graffiti wrought by bungling neoprene and fin. Free of bomb-fished coral ghettoes. Pristine. An Eden for sea life. Immersed in my world for two, we descend a steep and crusty coral wall stuck with a library of the soft, the calcareous, the prickly and the lichenous, all buzzing with a rush-hour of busying sea things. A bank of ecosystem fervour. Its frontage busy-bodies with crustacea and piscatorial neighbours: shrimps at their porches, eagerly dusting doorsteps with their fibrils; stripy sea slugs, all frills, ruffles, flutters and fibrillations – frivolous; rock lobsters anchored tight by their slippers; gorgonian fans, stuck like ritual Hindu offerings; gargantuan sponges, the size of plunge-tubs; a sea snake, venomous and zebra-striped, on the look-out for lunch; a turtle, rootling and patrolling, and a graceful eagle ray, that winged by like Concorde at a point where the current whipped over a cantilevered shelf and on to a roof garden. Pink, peach and cream table corals step the way, into an acid-dream world of Roger Dean gate-sleeve album covers ◙

Tales from topographic Oceans

A witch dances with eggs under her breasts through the
forests of the night.

STIR-FRIED VEGETABLES FOR NASI GORENG

Nasi goreng

Nasi goreng – fried rice – is the Bali basic that should be in everyone's handbook. A plus and minus dish, so use what you have. Cooked chicken or pork, egg (hard-boiled, fried or shredded omelette), salad, herbs, cucumber and tomato can all be used to dress nasi goreng. Here I've piled on some stir-fried greens. Nasi goreng is naked without its side dish of crisp rice crackers.

```
2 1/2 tbsp vegetable oil
6 small shallots, finely sliced
250g long-grain rice, freshly cooked and cooled
a handful each of stir-fryable greens, such as
  asparagus, mangetout, sugar snaps, beansprouts
salt and pepper
handful of prawn crackers, deep-fried in
  vegetable oil (optional)
```

Paste
```
2 cloves garlic, crushed
2 tsp shrimp paste, toasted
2 mild red chillies, chopped
1 tbsp kecap manis or dark soy sauce
1/2 tbsp sweet chilli sauce
```

For the dressing, in a mortar, pound together the garlic, shrimp paste and chillies, then mix in the kecap manis and chilli sauce. Or just chop and crush everything. Heat 2 tbsp oil in a wok or large frying pan and fry the shrimp paste mixture for 2 minutes. Add the shallots and stir-fry for about half a minute, then add the rice and stir-fry together for about 3 minutes. Divide between serving bowls or plates. Stir-fry the beansprouts and greens in 1/2 tbsp oil with salt and pepper for about 1 minute and pile on to the nasi goreng. Add rice crackers and egg, if there, and serve.

Sweet 'n sour sambal

Sambals (sauces) come with everything. This is close to a sambal petis, and is good with deep-fried battered vegetables – as in tempura – and anything grilled in fact. An excellent ketchup for takeaway. If you want to sharpen it up further, stir in a dash of rice vinegar.

```
8 red chillies, deseeded and chopped
1 tsp shrimp paste
3cm piece fresh galangal, peeled
  and chopped
4 shallots, chopped
4 cloves garlic
1 tbsp palm sugar or light brown sugar
2 tbsp oil
4 kaffir lime leaves, finely chopped
2 tbsp lime juice
```

Pound together all the ingredients, except the oil, lime leaves and juice, to make a coarse paste – or briefly blast in a processor. Fry in a wok in the oil until things start to look caramelized. Stir in the lime leaves, lime juice and 1 tbsp of water, bubble up, then leave to cool.

Temple rice parcels Lemper

Omigod. Banana leaves, glutinous rice, muslin and a steamer. Four beasts to find. So…. warning: do not attempt to make, unless you're up for a bit of fiddle and wrap – plus there's that elusive banana leaf to be harvested too. Fabulous my-aren't-you-clever party food – for those who want to recreate their Bali days, and unappease rival domestic gods/goddesses back home. To be authentic, stick some shredded dried beef in each packet. Asian shops are the places to pick up a packet of air-dried beef shreds, or use pounded shreds of South African biltong.

```
250g sticky (glutinous) rice, rinsed
250ml coconut milk
salt
1 banana leaf, cut into 8 large squares
```

Put the rice and coconut milk in a saucepan and simmer for 5-8 minutes, or until the milk is absorbed, but don't let it catch and burn. It will not be cooked at this point. Line a steamer tray with muslin, spread the rice on top and sprinkle with a little salt. Cover and fast-steam for about 25 minutes, then leave to cool. Divide the rice between the banana leaf squares and gently press into an oblong shaped layer, adding beef shreds, if using. Fold up the leaf into a tight parcel, folding in the ends and securing with bamboo or cocktail sticks. When wanted, grill over a barbecue or on a chargrill pan for about 4 minutes on each side.

COCONUT CRAB WATERCRESS SALAD, PAGE 233

Bali duck
Bebek batutu

In Ubud, they bake their bird whole and stuffed, and in the ground – wrapped in banana leaves and surrounded by smouldering coconut husks. No, I'm not suggesting it. This way below will give you that smoky flavour, and a full blast of the Moluccas, the spice islands. Not particularly Balinese, for ovens don't exist, but near. My nice easy way with a clutch of duck legs.

```
4 tbsp uncooked rice
4 1/2 tbsp palm sugar or soft brown
  sugar
4 cinnamon sticks, smashed
10 cloves, smashed
4 tbsp lapsang souchong tea leaves
4 duck legs
salt and pepper
1/2 tsp each of ground mace, cinnamon
  and cloves
1 tbsp kecap manis or dark soy sauce,
  for brushing
2 tbsp vegetable oil
```

Line the base of a steamer with a double thickness of foil. Mix together the uncooked rice, 4 tbsp of the sugar, the smashed cinnamon and cloves, and the tea leaves (the smoking ingredients), and spread over the foil. Assemble the steamer, placing the duck pieces in the steaming tray, then cover and place over a high heat. When you can smell the aroma of spice, turn down the heat to low and gently smoke for about 20 minutes. Discard the congealed smoking ingredients. Rub the now smoked duck with salt, pepper, the ground spices and the remaining 1/2 tbsp sugar, then brush with the kecap manis and some oil. Roast in a 190°C/375°F/Gas 5 oven on a baking sheet for about 40 minutes or until mahogany brown and cooked through. Eat with freshly cooked rice and some crisp leaves.

Seafood salad

Use those boiled pink seaside-type prawns in the shell here – they're cold-water goers and are sweet and juicy. Avoid the frozen peeled ones. Small tigers are fine too.

```
250g prepared baby squid tubes
300g shell-on cooked prawns
2 cloves garlic, chopped
2 small hot red chillies, deseeded and chopped
1/4 tsp shrimp paste or 1 tbsp fish sauce
```

Gado gado salad with peanut bumbu

To be Mr Authentic, you should blanch all the veg, then arrange them around a platter with sliced eggs on top, with the warmed dressing spooned over, and something crispy-fried on top. I go for crunchy and raw, like crudités. (See right).

```
selection of garden veg, cut to bite-size, such
  as radishes, sugar snaps, cauliflower, carrot,
  beansprouts, white cabbage or crisp salad leaves
8 quail's or 4 free-range hen's eggs, hard-boiled
  and sliced
prawn crackers, to serve
```

```
Peanut bumbu
1 clove garlic, chopped
2 shallots, sliced
3 small red chillies, finely chopped
1 tsp caster sugar
1 tbsp vegetable oil
1 tsp shrimp paste or 1 tbsp fish sauce
120g toasted crushed peanuts (see page 236)
250ml coconut cream (or coconut milk)
1 tbsp lime juice
```

Pound the garlic, shallots, chillies and sugar to a coarse paste, then fry it in the oil until softened. Stir in the shrimp paste or fish sauce and the peanuts and continue to fry for another minute, then pour in the coconut cream and 100ml water. Bubble up and cook until thick and peanut-butter-like. Stir in the lime juice and keep warm. Arrange the vegetables and eggs in bowls or on plates and serve with the warm peanut bumbu.

```
4 heaped tbsp sliced shallot
2 sticks lemongrass, trimmed and very
  finely sliced
salt
4 tbsp lemon or lime juice
1 tbsp palm sugar or caster sugar
1/2 small coconut, flesh grated
2 long red mild chillies, deseeded and
  finely shredded
4 kaffir lime leaves, finely shredded
a big handful each of mint and coriander
  leaves
```

Pop the squid tubes in a pan of boiling water and cook for about 1 minute, until cooked, then drain and leave to cool. De-shell the prawns and mix with the squid. Pound together the garlic, hot chillies, shrimp paste, 1 tbsp of the shallots and half the lemongrass with a pinch of salt to make a rough paste, then stir this into the lemon juice with the sugar. Toss this through the seafood and leave to marinate, covered and refrigerated, for a good hour. Toss through everything else and serve.

Crispy fish colo-colo

If deep-frying a fish sounds like hard work, grill it instead. The colo-colo sauce makes a spot-on dipping sauce for just about anything fried, battered or grilled that needs a good dunk. (See left).

1 large whole fish (freshwater or a sea fish, such as a snapper), scaled and gutted
salt
6 cloves garlic
5cm piece fresh root ginger, chopped
4 red birdseye chillies, deseeded and roughly chopped
4 large mild red chillies, deseeded and roughly chopped
3 tbsp caster sugar
5 tbsp fish sauce
5 tbsp lime juice
vegetable or sunflower oil

To serve
4 spring onions, shredded lengthways
handful of mint leaves
1 large mild red chilli, deseeded and finely shredded

Slash the fish through the flesh on both sides with diagonal cuts — five on each side — then rub all over with salt and put on one side. Pound the garlic, ginger and birdseye chillies with about 1 tsp of salt to make a paste. Crush the mild chillies into the paste, leaving them with a little texture. Stir in the sugar, fish sauce and about 2 tbsp water and spoon into a small pan. Bring the sauce to a boil, simmer gently until syrupy, then stir in the lime juice and leave to one side. Heat a deep pool of oil in a wok or pan, then test it with a cube of bread — it should fry and brown gently. Slip the fish into the hot oil (the oil may splash a little) and fry, turning once, until crisp and cooked — 5-8 minutes, depending on the size of your fish. Drain the fish and slip it on to a serving plate, then reheat the sauce and pour it over — and stick a thatch of the greenery and red chilli on top. Eat with rice.

Coconut crab watercress salad

Don't do crab? Use cooked prawns or squid instead. (See page 229).

2 cloves garlic, crushed
2 small hot red chillies, finely chopped
6 small (Thai) shallots, or 1 very small red onion, finely sliced
1 stick lemongrass, trimmed and very finely sliced
1 tbsp fish sauce
juice of 1 lemon
1 tbsp palm sugar or caster sugar
1 small young 'green' coconut, soft flesh scooped out (keep the water) — optional
100ml canned coconut cream or coconut milk
300g cooked white crab meat
1 long mild red chilli, deseeded and finely shredded
4 kaffir lime leaves, finely shredded
2 handfuls mixed mint and coriander leaves
1 big bunch watercress

Mix together the garlic, hot chillies, 1 tbsp of the shallots, lemongrass, fish sauce and lemon juice with the sugar and 2 tbsp of the coconut water (if you've kept it — or use water), then beat in the coconut cream. Toss this dressing through the crab meat and leave to marinate, covered and refrigerated, for a good hour. Gently fold the crab mixture through the remaining ingredients, including the remaining shallots and the coconut flesh (if using), and serve.

Beach-side gado gado

Simplicity. Well, beach-side stuff has to be. Some wizened kindly creature on an Ambon beach gave me this, pre-snorkel.

selection of prepared fruits, such as strips of green (unripe) mango, starfruit, cucumber and anything crunchy
1 raw sweet potato, peeled and cut into fine matchsticks

Dressing
1 clove garlic, sliced
1/2 tsp salt
2 small red chillies, finely chopped
2 tbsp palm sugar or soft brown sugar
100g toasted crushed peanuts (see page 236)
3 tsp kecap manis or dark soy sauce
juice of 2 small lemons or limes

Pound the garlic with the salt to a purée, add the chillies and crush further. Pound in the sugar and then the crushed toasted peanuts, kecap manis or soy sauce, and lemon or lime juice. Serve with the prepared sour fruits and sweet potato sticks.

Wok-fried chicken with beans, chilli and tamarind

3cm piece fresh root ginger, peeled
1 stick lemongrass, trimmed
2 cloves garlic
2 small hot red chillies
1 tsp salt
1 tsp shrimp paste
1 tsp caster sugar
4 free-range chicken breasts, skin on
coconut or groundnut oil
200g long beans, French beans or runner beans,
   topped, tailed, blanched and shredded
3 tbsp tamarind water (see page 236), or 2 tbsp
   lemon juice
2 handfuls whole/split toasted peanuts (see page 236)
2 long mild red chillies, shredded

Chop up the ginger, lemongrass, garlic and hot chillies, then pound to a paste with the salt, shrimp paste and sugar. Slice the chicken breasts into bite-sized chunks, then toss with the paste, cover, and leave on side to bathe for an hour or so. Heat a shallow pool of oil in a wok, then deep-fry the chicken pieces in batches until just cooked, about 3 minutes, depending on the size of your chunks. Drain. Decant most of the oil from the wok, then briefly stir-fry the shredded beans with a flick of salt, add the cooked chicken, tip in the tamarind and toss through. Toss in the peanuts and shredded chillies and serve.

Beef rendang curry

Beef rendang is not strictly Balinese, for they're all Hindu, and Hindus don't eat their cows. This one is more popular throughout the rest of the Indonesian islands – where buffalo is bunged into the pot. I don't expect you to find it – and beef works a treat here. A fabulous and easy curry. Leave it overnight, and things can only get better.

1kg stewing steak, cut into
   large chunks
3 tbsp vegetable oil
2 x 400ml cans coconut milk
8 kaffir lime leaves

Marinade
6 shallots, chopped
4 cloves garlic, chopped
3cm piece fresh root ginger, peeled
   and sliced
3cm piece fresh galangal, sliced
4 sticks lemongrass
4 hot red chillies, deseeded and
   finely chopped
salt

Pound together the marinade ingredients to make a coarse paste – or briefly blast in a processor. Rub this paste all over the beef, then leave refrigerated overnight.

Scrape off most of the paste and keep on one side. Fry the steak (in batches) in the oil in a casserole pan until browned on all sides. Remove from the pan and reserve. Put the coconut milk in a pan, bring to a boil, then slip the steak in with the reserved marinade gubbins and stir. Chuck in the lime leaves, then partially cover the pan and very gently stew for 2-2 1/2 hours or more, until the liquid has reduced and the beef is nice and tender. You must keep stirring though, or else it will catch and burn. It's safer to pop it in the oven (something around 160°C/325°F/Gas 3), with a lid – but leave it askew, for the sauce must reduce – and give it a stir through every now and then. Add a dash of water if things get too dry before the beef is done. It gets even better if now left overnight and then reheated – with a dash more of the coconut milk or water – the next day. Eat with rice.

Lombok lemongrass and chilli chicken

You could do this with your eyes shut. So, wheel on the barbie and slip the gamelan CD on, and grill to the sounds of Bali's haunting bronze gongs, drums and xylophones in full ringing swing. Serve with salad, lime wedges and, if you're up for it, the sambal on page 227. Lombok, by the way, is Bali's neighbouring island.

2 poussins (small chickens), or
  8 chicken thighs
salt
1 tsp caster sugar
3 shallots, chopped
2 sticks lemongrass, trimmed and
  chopped
2 cloves garlic, chopped
3cm piece fresh root ginger, peeled
  and chopped
4 red chillies, deseeded and chopped
vegetable oil

To serve
crisp salad leaves and lime wedges

Spatchcock the chicken by cutting out the backbone and flattening the birds out, then make light slashes through the meat. If using thighs, slash them only. Pound together all the ingredients, except the chicken and oil — or blast in a processor until finely chopped. Smother over the flattened chicken and leave to bathe for a couple of hours or overnight. Brush the chicken with oil and grill over hot coals for 10-15 minutes on each side, or until cooked through when tested with the point of a knife. If using thighs, grill them for around 8 minutes on each side. Eat with salad.

Tofu with chunky tomato sambal

If tofu is not you, serve the sambal with fried, grilled or roasted chicken instead. In Bali they'd use tempe (soybean cake). The sambal is similar to one known as pecel – and when served with fried catfish, it's pecel lele (sound familiar? Piccalilli, I'm sure of it).

500g tofu or tempe, cut into squares
  and drained
salt
plain flour, for dusting
vegetable oil

Tomato sambal
1 stick lemongrass, trimmed and
  finely chopped
3 red chillies, finely sliced
1 clove garlic, crushed
1 tsp shrimp paste
vegetable oil
3 tsp palm sugar or caster sugar
4 tomatoes, deseeded and
  roughly chopped
2 tbsp kecap manis or dark soy sauce
4 tbsp tamarind water (see page
  236), or 2 tbsp lemon juice and
  2 tbsp water
2 tbsp toasted crushed peanuts (see
  page 236)

To make the sambal, mix together the lemongrass, chillies, garlic and shrimp paste and fry in 1 tbsp oil for about 1 minute. Stir in the remaining ingredients, apart from the peanuts, and leave to cool. To cook the drained tofu or tempe, season the squares with some salt and dust with flour, then fry in a pool of oil in a wok until crisp and golden. Drain. Serve the sambal spooned over the tofu, or by itself in a small dish, both sprinkled with crushed toasted peanuts.

Asia Basics

Toasted crushed peanuts

Spread unsalted skinned peanuts over a roasting
tin and roast in a 200°C/400°F/Gas 6 oven for
about 10 minutes, shaking the tin occasionally to
turn them, until golden all over. Once cooled a
bit, crush them in a mortar. They'll keep like
this sealed in a tub for a good month, so make
extra if you make lots of South-East Asiany things.

Toasted ground rice

Toast 4 tbsp uncooked rice in a
heavy, hot frying pan until golden
brown all over - keep shaking the
pan so that it doesn't catch and
burn. Next, tip out of the pan and
leave the rice to cool, then whizz
in a coffee grinder to a fine powder.

Tamarind water

User-friendly tamarind paste in
a jar is fast becoming available
with instructions on the label. If
it's a block you're dealing with,
then here's how: put 50g block
tamarind in a bowl and add 150ml
kettle-boiled water to just cover.
Leave until it turns pasty (about
an hour), then break it up with a
fork. To speed the softening
process, you could simmer it for
around 10 minutes. Tip the mixture
into a sieve sat over another bowl,
pushing through as much of the mush
as possible. Discard the pod and
seed gunk left in the sieve and
keep the thick juice.

Perfect steam-boiled rice

For perfect steam-boiled rice, put your
washed rice (the speediest method is to
let the cold water tap jet through it in a
sieve) into a saucepan and level, then
pour in enough water to come about 2cm
above the rice. To gauge this, stick your
forefinger in until it just touches the
rice - the distance between the tip and
the first joint of your finger is the
correct measure. So, no rulers please.
Bring to a bubble, salt it well, and allow
to boil for 2 minutes, then turn down the
heat to extremely low, cover and simmer for
8 minutes. Turn off the heat and leave,
covered, for a further 10 minutes.
Fluff through.

Asian fish cake

In a processor, pulse to a paste
250g skinned and boned white fish
fillet with 1/2 tsp of salt, a
touch of msg (if you do) and 2 tsp
of cornflour. Knead together,
slapping it against the side of the
bowl to knock out any air. Mould
the paste into a 2cm-thick
rectangular slab, then slip into
the fridge, covered, to firm up.
Cut into wide strips, coat each in
cornflour, dip in a lightly beaten
egg, then fry straight away a
shallow pool of vegetable oil (a
wok is good) until golden on all
sides. Cool, then slice. It will
reheat once it meets the dish it's
chucked in to.

Asian soup stock

Break up a left-over chicken carcass into
bits or chop 2 chicken pieces into chunks,
bones and all. Stick the bits in a largish
saucepan, add around 2-litres of water and
give it a good salting. Bring to a bubble
and spoon off any gunky stuff that floats
to the top, then sling in 5cm peeled and
thickly sliced fresh root ginger and 5
halved and chopped fat spring onions. Turn
down the heat and leave to bubble gently
for about 1 hour. Strain the stock and
discard all the bones and bits.

Thai red curry paste

Various ready-made red Thai curry pastes are on the scene now (the Thai Nam
Jai brand is particularly good), but for true die-hard curry-ites, heres how to
make your own.

De-seed 6 long red dried chillies and 4 small red birdseye
chillies, then roughly chop. Chop up 4 shallots, 8 cloves garlic,
and 2 peeled sticks of lemon grass, 5 cm root ginger and the same
of galangal (or extra root ginger), then pound these with the
chillies to a paste. If using a mortar and pestle, start by
pounding the firmer things, then work in the more delicate toward
the end and, if things start to look too full, do in batches.
Alternatively pulverise the lot in the processor. Next, pound 6
finely chopped lime leaves - or the finely grated zest of 1/2 a
lime, 3 tsp shrimp paste (or add 2 tbsp fish sauce when adding the
oil at the end) and 1 tsp coriander seeds - or a few chopped fresh
coriander roots, if your bunch has them. Then bind the lot
together with a tablespoon of oil. It should have texture and
some fibre about it. Leftover paste will keep for a good week or
so refrigerated.

Picture captions

p1 Disposable toothbrush and paste from The Dan Chu Hotel, Hanoi, Vietnam.

p2,3 Dawn in Mrauk U, one of Burma's ancient capitals, that lies crumbling under vines and jungle on an isolated plateau in the state of Arakan, West Myanmar. Its temples are shrouded by mists and the smoke from early morning fires.

p4 A traditional boat with hand-stitched sail works one of Kerala's backwater lagoons near Cochin, India.

p5 A Thai spoon and chopstick box holds the family cutlery.

India

p8 A women samples the quality of the flower heads, used for ritual purposes, at Mumbai's (Bombay) flower markets.

p10 A tin platter of juvenile breakwater fish, caught by Fort Cochin's Chinese fishing nets. Once rubbed with spice and fried until crisp – heads, tails, fins and all – they're piled with lime-drenched slivers of red onion and hot green chillies and eaten with cool yoghurt.

p11 A boy with religious face paint at Crawford Market, Bombay, one of India's busiest markets.

p12 A traditional spice box from Jaisalmere in Rajasthan holds (from top, left to right) chilli, green cardamom, cinnamon sticks, black peppercorns, ground turmeric and coriander seeds.

p14,15 Evening waters roll in from the Malabar Banks, churning the brackish waters and weeds that lap the towering, creaking Chinese fishing nets, built by ancient traders from the court of Kublai Khan. Fort Cochin, Kerala.

p16 Male elephants, adorned with gold brow and face plates, follow in the wake of musicians with drums, clarinets, cymbals and horns, at a Hindu temple festival in the month of Virchikam (Nov/Dec) at Tripunithura – their riders atop with parasols, fans and pom-pom paraphernalia. Original gold masks were sold by the East India Company to pay for Kochi's railway, and now only the central plates remain. Tusks are kept trimmed, shaped and polished specially.

p18,19 Washing-up bowls stacked with seafood are massed between the fish stalls and the tide at Fort Cochin, Kerala: steely fry and mullet; aquarium-like Athena fish; inky baskets of squid, turquoise mussels; and fat blue prawns. Larger fish: baby hammerhead sharks; torpedo-shaped tuna; and razor-sharp barracuda, laze out on tables. Two-man operated long boats chunter on in, bringing it by the basketful all day.

p25 A fisherman casts his line on Cochin's backwaters.

p30 Things reach a fruity fever pitch in May in the lofty halls of Crawford Market, Mumbai (Bombay). It's a big 46°C around town and peak Alphonso mango harvest time. The old Victorian pillared veg market heaves with the fruits. Crates upon crates packed with straw stack the dark halls and line the tarpaulin-slung stalls. The neat rows of golden-yellow little orbs spill with acid sweetness. Everyone trots this way and that with big wheel-sized baskets on their heads.

p31 The ringed toes of a woman at the Mahila Mandal: a ladies co-op, set up 30 years ago for the widowed and handicapped, and for those dumped or abused by drug-addicted husbands. The co-op's primary aim is, to quote their booklet, "to help our needy sisters, to create in them a feeling of self-confidence, self-empowerment and a will to mould their lives and those of their children".

Burma

p34 Votive candles burn around old Rangoon's 98-metre-high golden dome of Shwedagon Paya, the most sacred and eleborate of Buddhist sites in Burma, which was rebuilt in 1769, after yet another earthquake had cast it a heavy blow. "A beautiful winking wonder" Kipling called it. North-central Yangon.

p36 An Intha fisherman quietly and methodically stalks fish that lurk in the tangled dark depths of Inle Lake, Shan State, Eastern Burma. Once he's caught the flicker of a breath on the surface, he sends down his bamboo-framed cone-shaped net to catch the life below.

p37 Nga-hpein (a type of carp), caught from Inle Lake, is weighed out for a shopper at Indain Market.

p38 Pickled beansprouts and greens, coriander and sliced cucumber accompany many Burmese curries.

p42, 43 Tea at Indain Market, a short boat ride through floating gardens, lotus and bamboo clumps, from Inle Lake.

p44 A boy novice monk appears from his monastery dormitory at Inle Lake.

p45 A stone buddha sits in one of Bagan's temple alcoves, one in a cast of thousands that inhabit a labyrinth of temple tunnels; now fallen worlds, knitted together by root and tuft.

p46 A Pa hoh tribeswoman sips tea in Kalaw's hill station market at one of the eating stalls. The best is Aung Nyein Chan Aung Restaurant. Hardly a restaurant. A shoe-box kitchen, clean and neat, and some tables where they serve Shan noodles, Bamar food: noodles tossed with niblets of pork, chicken and spring onion, topped with crisp noodle for crunch, plus pickles, and a bowl of clear greens soup, as standard.

p49 A Gaungbaung tribesman (identified by his coloured towelling headgear, wrapped turban-style like an out-sized sweatband) puffs on a cheroot at Nam Pan Market, Inle Lake.

p50 Fresh fish at market.

p51 Traders and shoppers get ready to disembark from their boat on Inle Lake for Nam Pan Market. Moke kyut (rice crackers), pressed beancurd, and vast banana leaf-lined baskets of steaming cooked rice are unloaded.

p52 A Burmese girl applies her bark paste face paint (thanaka). The fine paste acts as a sun-block and moisturizer and tightens up the skin.

p53 Dawn over Mrauk U's hilly terrain. The spires pierce the low-lying mists and the smoke of fires, making this one of the most magical dawns on Earth.

p54 Reflection. Fish plop, dragonflies hum and Insecta buzz all day long around waters dappled with Hockney squiggles and abstractions aplenty. Inle Lake is the place of escape.

p56 The sun sets behind Sulamani Phato – brick-built pinnacles to the virtuous, to aspiration. With its Sleeping Beauty towers, it's Bagan's crown at sunset.

p58 The sun sinks over the ancient kingdom of Bagan and melts into the boiling oil of day-end colour. Palm, tree and spire become silhouettes.

p59 A boy takes his evening wash with water poured from a watering can at Mrauk U's main temple plain.

p63 Sunset at Ngapali Beach.

p72 Women saunter with aluminium water pots (imported from India) permanently attached, like handbags, yet cradled on a hip. They pass, posture perfect, along dirt walkways shaded by banana, betel and coconut palm. Mrauk U.

p73 A stop at Myanmu, half-way down the Ayeyerwady River, and gang-planks are thrown down, there's more green banana loading, and the samosa and watermelon girls pile on – to be herded off as we pull out again.

Thailand

p76 Soft pink and blue waterlillies, along with roses and orchids, are a Thai's choice of flowers.

p78 Smoke hangs over the waters, houseboats and stilted homes of the Thonburi waterways – a maze of old canals that leads off Bangkok's Chao Phraya River.

p78 The salt of nam pla (fish sauce made from fermented anchovies) steeps the shadows. Nam pla is a Thai's table salt, and it's splashed over everything in quantites we westerners would flinch at.

p80 Glass noodles are wrapped into spring rolls and deep fried, then eaten wrapped with sweet basil and lettuce leaves and dunked in nam jim kai (a dipping sauce made from rice vinegar and hot chilli sauce).

p82 A monk leaves his sleeping quarters.

p83 A street stall table, after lunch.

p84,85 Incense sticks burn in droves in temples, adding their perfume to this land of fragrance. Wat Po, Bangkok.

p86 Lotus leaves.

p87 Sen yai (fresh wide-line noodles) are stirred into chicken or pork bone-simmered broths that are flavoured with lemongrass, spring onion and garlic chives. This broth, kaeng jeut, is a bland restorative comfort noodle soup.

p88 Hot, sweet, salty and sour wraps, mien kum, are sold by hawkers in their components, neatly poly-bagged in kit form, for home assembly.

p91 A woman at the talaat naam (water market) in Ratchaburi, her boat kitted out as a kitchen, spoons and ladles with dexterity patterned by years of repeat. All around a delicious steam, sauced by nam pla, builds into the morning air.

p92 A monk paddles up-river, collecting alms of rice and curry. He works his way along the ton-chak (water palm) thicketed khlongs of Samut Songkhram province.

p95 Women gossip at Talaat Ton Khem floating market, in boats laden with baskets of artfully arranged things. Money changes hands midstream, and melons and mangoes swap craft.

p96,97 Anchovies are dried on mesh racks in the sun. The fish are brought in at the port of Samaesan, near Pattaya.

p100 A bowl of steaming goodness. Noodles, fish balls and crispy dried shrimp are dressed with chopsticks and spoon to land with a flourish into a waiting hand. Spoonfuls of chilli-ringed fish sauce are then spooned on. Talaat Ton Khem floating market, on the Damnoen Saduak canal (104km south-west of Bangkok in Ratchaburi province).

p101 Coconut palm silhouette.

p105 Thin cut rice noodles(sen mee).

p108 A fresh catch of blue tiger prawns on sale at the Chang Pier's forecourt (next to the Royal Palace gardens), Bangkok, which leads to the Chao Phya River. Here hawkers set up in the calm of a breeze under trees heavy with frangipane scent. Steam idles in drifts and oil muffles as battered morsels hit well-tuned pans.

p109 Women work the waters in the cool of early morning at Talaat Ton Khem floating market, on the Damnoen Saduak canal in the Ratchaburi province.

p111 The tall fronds of Ton-chak (water palm) hedge the khlongs.

Laos

p120 Chinese tea cups. Many Indo-Chinese enjoy food and drinks common to China.

p122 A sikhara, the gilded metal tiered crown that tops many a sacred stupa (religous monument).

p123 Wat Xieng Thong is the Luang Prabang's prettiest temple. At 500 years old, it's one of the city's oldest, and is akin in design to the northern Siamese or Lanna style. Rooves sweep low and are layered, like a mother hen guarding her chicks, say the Laos.

p124 Slices of cucumber accompany many Laoation meals. The mix of salty, hot, sour, bitter and sweet must have its counterbalancers of cool and crunch.

p128 On the outskirts of town in Luang Prabang, salad gardens are laid down in quilts of lushness – complete with stream, and narrow mud paths for small feet. Gardeners pick and plant, tend and care, weed and water, obsessed.

p129 A basket of freshly picked coriander is taken to the stream to be washed.

p130 Neatly wrapped banana leaf packages, holding small noodle-tossed lunches, rice and grilled meat, can be had from Talaat Naviengkham morning market in Luang Prabang.

p131 Each morning at dawn, the pound of pestle on mortar can be heard from behind shuttered doors, kettles emit steam on fires, and the novice monks pass barefoot, come rain or shine, through streets and collect their alms.

p132 Oyster mushrooms.

p133 The Mekong, as seen on top of Luang Prabang's central peak, Phu Si (the place for sunset views), turns to silver at sundown, and glides away effortlessly and vast, ribboning off through folds of dark green.

p134 River boats moored up on The Mekong.

p137 Baskets of chillies at Talaat Naviengkham morning market.

p138 A monk cleans his alms dishes at the window of his monastary room, at Wat Sirumungkhun, Luang Prabang.

p146 A monk with his pot.

p147 Traditional knives bought from a street stall are wrapped in recycled paper and bound with twine.

Vietnam

p152 A bowl of noodles laced with beansprouts and herbage is passed to a customer at Hué's Hang Da morning market, by the Perfume River.

p154 Shoppers tuck into lunch at a stall outside Hoi An's market by The Bon River.

p155 Inscription on a plaque placed on a tomb in the Chi Khiem Temple at the Tomb of Tu Duc outside Hué.

p156 Rice noodles and fragrant stock form the base of many a one-bowl meal.

p160 A hill tribe boy downs breakfast at Bac Ha Market, Lao Cai province, Northern Vietnam. Leaf soups steeped with celery are doled out, mounded with minced pork or chicken; and tofu tumbled in stock is doused with mint, chilli flakes and rings of orange chilli fished from nuoc mam (fish sauce).

p161 For the home cook who strives to cut corners, green beens come ready-sliced at Hué's Hang Da morning market.

p162 Chopsticks, ready to go.

p163 Everyone scoffs with blind concentration at Bac Ha's Market, where buffalos and pigs are traded amid a lot of push and shove.

p165 A Dao tribe girl carries, back-pack style, a woven basket loaded with wood gathered from the forest.

p166 Pho ga (chicken, noodles, beansprouts and herbs doused with a good squirt of lime) is breakfast at Bac Ha's market. A scant bit of bird cleaved with bones and all, and delicious.

p168 A H'mong tribeswoman tucks in, amidst the steam of bubbling pans and the drift of pork-fat smoke, at Sapa's covered market. The blue stain from dying clothes clings to her finger nails.

p169 Backdrops are brushed lush with chameorops fan palms

p170, 171 A Hanoi cyclist in cooli hat. Everything and everyone goes by bike around Vietnam. .

p174 A hawker makes her way through the narrow streets of Hoi An. It's a laid-back place, where car-free streets, old shuttered houses and alleys lead down to The Bon River, where houseboats moor.

p175 Bamboo at sunset.

p183 There's always someone parked-up somewhere with charcoal smoking. This woman grills bamboo-threaded, lemongrass-marinaded beef over charcoal, then serves it wrapped up with its customery mint, basil and saw-tooth coriander leafage, plus slivers of star fruit, in a neat rice paper roll in Hoi An.

p184 A cross-pole hawker carries water spinach (rau muong), Vietnam's most ubiquitous national vegetable. Adored for its crunchy stem and soft leaves, it's an aquatic plant, and is most often stir-fried.

Singapore

p192 Prosperity characters written on a shop wall.

p194 Lanterns hang from the eaves of a shop front in Singapore's Chinatown.

p195 The fish ball noodle counter at Kuan's restaurant fronts the pavement at the junction of Keong Saik and Bridge St., Chinatown.

p196 Soy sauce and black salted beans

p200 A pot of jasmine tea is obligatory with dim sum

p208 Rice noodles are strained in a spider (a basket spoon) and quickly aired and separated with cook's chopsticks.

p209 A street vendor sells duck noodle soup. Shelves of noodles fill his cabinet, and lettuces swing by roasted ducks.

Bali

p214 Ritual flower heads.

p216 The crater lake at Bratan, Northern central Bali, a magical and serene mirror-glass of water, is home to the goddess of irrigation, Dewi Danau, and a thatched seventeenth-century lake-side pagoda Buddhist temple (Pura Ulun Danau).

p217 Tofu with chunky tomato sambal. Sambals are hot and spicy relishes, and come with everything.

p222 Rice paddy.

p224 Palm leaf and hibiscus offerings are placed to the gods at doorways and temples, to appease the demon underworld. Agama Hindu is practised, devotion to one supreme god, Sanghyang Widi, plus the embodiment of the Hindu trinity of Brahma, Vishnu and Siva.

p225 Sundown view of the volcano, Gunung Agung that rises 3142 metres over the north-eastern corner of the island, as seen from the Bedugal Hotel.

p228 Custard apples.

Index

Ambon (Indonesia) 223, 233
aubergine
    pork dumpling, aubergine and salt-fish hotpot 204
    smoky aubergine with coriander and chilli 190
    Temple aubergine with sweet chilli shrimp sauce 142
Ayeyerwady River (Burma (Myanmar)) 47

Bagan (Burma (Myanmar)) 47-8
Balachong 69
Bali 214-35
    flavours 219-21
banana leaves
    banana leaf grilled mackerel 189
    Temple rice parcels 227
Banda Besa (Indonesia) 223
Bandaneira (Indonesia) 223
Bangkok 89, 114
    Bangkok chicken rice plate 117
beans
    dim sum ribs with salted black beans 205
    wok-fried chicken with beans, chilli and tamarind 234
beansprouts, pickled 61
beef
    barbecue beef with starfruit (banh cuon) 190
    beef rendang 234
bhel puri 28
Bombay (Mumbai) 27, 28
Burma (Myanmar) 34-75
    flavours 39-41

caramel
    caramel pork and prawns with pickled greens 184
    toasted caramel dipping sauce 151
Cardamom Hill rice 26
cashew, lime and spring onion stir-fry 141
Chang Pier (Bangkok) 89

Chang Pier noodle salad 106
chapatis 27
Chatujak market (Bangkok) 89
Chatujak satay 102
chicken
    Bangkok chicken rice plate 117
    in Chatujak satay 102
    chicken and mint salad 180
    chicken and mushroom soup 112
    in comfort noodle soup 99
    green chilli chicken 33
    Hanoi chicken noodle soup (pho ga) 184
    Hill station chicken curry with new potatoes (Burmese) 74
    Lombok lemongrass and chilli chicken 235
    Nonya pot-braised chicken 212
    Railway station chicken 64
    sticky ginger chicken wings with herbs 185
    tandooried chicken 27
    wok-fried chicken with basil and chilli 98
    wok-fried chicken with beans, chilli and tamarind 234
chilli
    chilli salt and lime grilled corn-on-the-cob 28
    green chilli chicken 33
    lime and chilli butter clams with baguette 189
    Lombok lemongrass and chilli chicken 235
    mussels with ginger and chilli 23
    Ngapali Beach chilli crab 74
    octopus, chilli and herb salad 64
    smoky aubergine with coriander and chilli 190
    sweet chilli shrimp sauce 142
    wok-fried basil and chilli chicken 98
    wok-fried chicken with beans, chilli and tamarind 234
chutney
    coconut and mint chutney 21
    green chutney 21

thali chutney 21
    see also pickles
Cochin 17
coconut
    coconut crab watercress salad 233
    coconut fish curry 102
    coconut and mint chutney 21
    coconut sambal 32
coriander, smoky aubergine with coriander and chilli 190
corn-on-the-cob
    chilli salt and lime grilled 28
    see also sweetcorn
crab
    black pepper crab with curry leaves 212
    coconut crab watercress salad 233
    crab and sweetcorn soup 213
    Ngapali Beach chilli crab 74
    stir-fried crab claws 114
cucumber, Hué prawn and cucumber salad 185
curry
    beef rendang 234
    coconut fish curry 102
    green ginger river prawn curry 75
    Hill station chicken curry with new potatoes 74
    lamb curry 67
    prawn and mango curry 33
    Thai red curry paste 237
curry leaves
    black pepper crab with curry leaves 212
    curry leaf shrimp 32

dim sum
    dim sum duck noodle soup 204
    dim sum mushrooms 205
    dim sum ribs with salted black beans 205
dressings
    for beach-side gado gado 233
    for Luang Prabang garden salad 148
    see also sauces
duck

Bali duck 230
    braised duck rice 211
    dim sum duck noodle soup 204
dumplings, pork dumpling, aubergine and salt-fish hotpot 204

eggs
    in gado gado salad with peanut bumbu 230
    in Luang Prabang garden salad 148
fish
    banana leaf grilled mackerel 189
    broken fish trap 112
    cha ca (grilled fish with noodles) 172, 179
    coconut fish curry 102
    crispy fish colo-colo 233
    fish ball noodle 210
    fish cake 237
    in floating market noodles (soup) 115
    garam masala whitebait with lime, yoghurt and mint 26
    lemongrass fish salad with chilli and lime 141
    Malabar fish pilaff with raisins, cardamom, pepper and mace 23
    pork dumpling, aubergine and salt-fish hotpot 204
Fransipan Mountain (Vietnam) 164

gado gado
    Beach-side gado gado 233
    gado gado salad with peanut bumbu 230
garam masala
    garam masala whitebait with lime, yoghurt and mint 26
    as ingredient 27
garlic
    Chandrika's garlic pickle 21
    stove-grilled jumbo prawns with 20 garlic cloves 28
ginger
    ginger squid salad 185
    green ginger river prawn curry 75

Keralan mussels with ginger and chilli 23
sticky ginger chicken wings with herbs 185
Halong Bay (Vietnam) 167
Hang Da market (Hué) 172, 184
Hanoi 159, 167, 172
  Hanoi chicken noodle soup (pho ga) 184
Hoi An (Vietnam) 190
Hué (Vietnam) 173
  Hué prawn and cucumber salad 185

ice-cream, saffron ice-cream 26
India 8-33
  flavours 13
Indonesia 214-35
  flavours 219-21
Inle Lake (Burma (Myanmar)) 67

Jaisalmer 26

keema fry with mint and flatbreads 27
Kerala 23
khlong tom yam 99

lamb curry, Burmese 67
Laos 120-51
  flavours 125-7
lassi, with saffron ice-cream 26
Lay Myo River (Burma (Myanmar)) 75
lemongrass
  lemongrass fish salad with chilli and lime 141
  Lombok lemongrass and chilli chicken 235
  in lime and chilli butter clams with baguette 189
  Lombok lemongrass and chilli chicken 235
Luang Prabang (Laos) 135-6, 141, 151
  Luang Prabang garden salad 148

maize see corn-on-the-cob; sweetcorn
Malabar 17, 23
Mandalay Hill (Burma (Myanmar)) 69
mango
  prawn and mango curry 33
  spiced mango dip 21
marinade, for beef rendang 234
Maymyo Hill Station (Burma (Myanmar)) 74
Mekong River
  Laos 125, 135
  Vietnam 157
Moluccas (Indonesia) 219, 230
Mount Popa (Burma (Myanmar)) 47-8, 61
Mrauk U (Burma (Myanmar)) 47-8
Mumbai (Bombay) 27, 28
mushroom
  chicken and mushroom soup 112
  dim sum mushrooms 205
  hot and sour oyster mushroom and pumpkin soup 151
  in Vietnamese spring rolls 180
  wok mushrooms and greens 211
Myanmar see Burma (Myanmar)
Myanmu (Burma (Myanmar)) 47

naan bread 27
nam jim, with glass noodle spring rolls 98
nam jim kai la (dipping sauce) 89
Nam Khan River (Laos) 135, 141
nam pla 81, 89
Ngapali Beach (Burma (Myanmar)) 70, 74
Nonya pot-braised chicken 212
noodles
  in banana leaf grilled mackerel 189
  cao lau noodles 177
  cha ca (grilled fish with noodles)

172, 179
Chang Pier noodle salad 106
comfort noodle soup 99
dim sum duck noodle soup 204
fish ball noodle 210
floating market noodles 115
glass noodles 89, 98, 106
Hanoi chicken noodle soup (pho ga) 184
in Joo Chiat prawn laksa with dill 210
Mandalay Hill noodles 69
in prawn chow mein 213
Shan noodles 75

octopus/squid
Best friend squid salad 70
in Chang Pier noodle salad 106
dipping squid hotpot 177
ginger squid salad 185
in Night fisherman's soup 70
octopus, chilli and herb salad 64
in seafood salad 230

papaya
green papaya and peanut salad 114
green papaya salad 61
spicy green papaya salad with basil and mint 145
parathas 27
peanuts
peanut bumbu 230
toasted crushed peanuts 236
pickles
Chandrika's garlic pickle 21
pickled beansprouts 61
pickled radish and greens 69
see also chutney
pooris (puris) 21
bhel puri 28
poppadums 21
pork
pork with cao lau noodles 177
caramel pork and prawns with pickled greens 184
in Chang Pier noodle salad 106
dim sum ribs with salted black beans 205
pork dumpling, aubergine and salt-fish hotpot 204
roast pork and clam sticky rice 205
in Shan noodles 75
in Vietnamese spring rolls 180
prawns/shrimps
Balachong 69
in broken fish trap (tom yam) 112
caramel pork and prawns with pickled greens 184
curry leaf shrimp 32
in floating market noodles (soup) 115
green ginger river prawn curry 75
in green papaya and peanut salad 115
Hué prawn and cucumber salad 185
Joo Chiat prawn laksa with dill 210
in jungle tiger salad 118
in khlong tom yam 99
prawn chow mein 213
prawn and mango curry 33
in seafood salad 230
shrimp paste 81
stove-grilled jumbo prawns with 20 garlic cloves 28
sweet chilli shrimp sauce 142
in Vietnamese spring rolls 180
pumpkin, hot and sour oyster mushroom and pumpkin soup 151

radish, pickled radish and greens 69
Rangoon (Yangon) 64
Ratchaburi province (Thailand) 94
red onion salad 21

Red River (Vietnam) 157, 164, 167
rice
Bangkok chicken rice plate 117
braised duck rice 211
Cardamom Hill rice 26
fish pilaff 23
Laos sticky rice 145
nasi goreng (fried rice) 227
roast pork and clam sticky rice 205
steam boiled rice 236
steamed rice pancakes (banh cuon) 172, 190
Temple rice parcels 227
toasted ground rice 236
toasted rice crackers (banh da) 185
rijsttafel 223
roti 27

saffron ice-cream 26
salad
Best friend squid salad 70
Chang Pier noodle salad 106
chicken and mint salad 180
coconut crab watercress salad 233
gado gado salad with peanut bumbu 230
ginger squid salad 185
green papaya salad 61
green papaya and peanut salad 114
green tomato salad 61
Hué prawn and cucumber salad 185
Jungle tiger salad 118
lemongrass fish salad with chilli and lime 141
Luang Prabang garden salad 148
octopus, chilli and herb salad 64
red onion salad 21
seafood salad 230
spicy green papaya salad with basil and mint 145
sambal
chunky tomato sambal 235
coconut sambal 32
sweet 'n sour sambal 227
Samut Songkhram province (Thailand) 93-4
Sapa (Vietnam) 164-7
satay, Chatujak satay 102
sauces
chunky tomato sambal 235
coconut sambal 32
colo-colo 233
dipping sauce (Burma) 64
dipping sauce (Laos) 151
dipping sauce (nam jim kai la) (Thailand) 89
dipping sauce (nuoc cham) (Vietnam) 180, 185
dipping sauce (Thailand) 117
padaek (fish sauce) 127, 145
peanut jam sauce 118
sweet chilli shrimp sauce 142
sweet 'n sour sambal 227
toasted caramel dipping sauce (Laos) 151
see also dressings
sausage, Vietnamese sausage (nem) 185
seafood see crab; fish; octopus/squid; prawns/shrimps; shellfish
Semeikhon (Burma (Myanmar)) 47
shellfish
Keralan mussels with ginger and chilli 23
lime and chilli butter clams with baguette 189
roast pork and clam sticky rice 205
shrimps see prawns/shrimps
Singapore 192-213
flavours 197
soup
Asian soup stock 237
chicken and mushroom soup 112

comfort noodle soup 99
crab and sweetcorn soup 213
dim sum duck noodle soup 204
floating market noodles 115
green leaf soup 179
Hanoi chicken noodle soup (pho ga) 184
hot and sour oyster mushroom and pumpkin soup 151
khlong tom yam 99
Night fisherman's soup (Burma) 70
spring rolls
crispy spring rolls (Vietnamese) 180
glass noodle spring rolls with nam jim (Thai) 98
squid see octopus/squid
starfruit, barbecue beef with starfruit (banh cuon) 190
stir-fry
cashew, lime and spring onion stir-fry 141
stir-fried crab claws 114
Sulamani Phato (Burma (Myanmar)) 47-8
Sulawesi (Indonesia) 223
sweetcorn
crab and sweetcorn soup 213
see also corn-on-the-cob

Talaat Khem floating market (Thailand) 94
tamarind, wok-fried chicken with beans, chilli and tamarind 234
tamarind water 236
tandooried chicken 27
Thailand 76-119
flavours 81
Thandwe market (Burma (Myanmar)) 64
tofu, with chunky tomato sambal 235
tomatoes
chunky tomato sambal 235
green tomato salad 61
in Luang Prabang garden salad 148

Ubud (Indonesia) 230

Vietnam 152-91
flavours 157-9

watercress
coconut crab watercress salad 233
in Luang Prabang garden salad 148
watercress wraps, hot, sweet, salty and sour 118

yoghurt
yoghurt dip 21
as ingredient 26

Thank you to:

Becca, Susan and both Tims.
Kate, Kit and Yuki.
India: Dr Thampi and The Spices Board of India, plus The United Nations Development Projects Fund, and Mr Jamaludeen and Mr Vareesh; Meena Patak and Lucie Moran.
Burma: Tha Zan Maung, and Kyaw Swa Linn (Jo); and MiMi for coming to the rescue. Vietnam: Mr Chung at the Dan Chu Hotel, Miss Chi and the Hanoi British Embassy, and Nicki Rowntree; Laos: Ivan Scholte; Thailand: Blue Dragon and Mr Boonpud; and to Lonely Planet. For all places to eat and stay mentioned in this book, and for further information on the dos and don'ts of travel – what to take and what to not, and more, contact
www.foodfromourtravels.com